FUHGEDDABOUDIT!

FUHGEDDABOUDIT!

FROM FIST-PUMPING
to the Family Restaurant

101 WAYS TO TELL IF YOU'RE A *REAL* GUIDO

ANDREA RENZONI AND ERIC RENZONI

Avon, Massachusetts

Copyright © 2010 by F+W Media, Inc.
All rights reserved.
This book, or parts thereof, may not be reproduced in any
form without permission from the publisher; exceptions are
made for brief excerpts used in published reviews.
Published by
Adams Media, a division of F+W Media, Inc.
57 Littlefield Street, Avon, MA 02322. U.S.A.
www.adamsmedia.com

ISBN 10: 1-4405-0661-2
ISBN 13: 978-1-4405-0661-1
eISBN 10: 1-4405-0870-4
eISBN 13: 978-1-4405-0870-7

Printed in the United States of America.

10   9   8   7   6   5   4   3   2   1

Library of Congress Cataloging-in-Publication Data
Renzoni, Andrea.
Fuhgeddaboudit! / Andrea Renzoni and Eric Renzoni.
p. cm.
ISBN-13: 978-1-4405-0661-1
ISBN-10: 1-4405-0661-2
ISBN-13: 978-1-4405-0870-7 (electronic)
ISBN-10: 1-4405-0870-4 (electronic)
1.Italian Americans—Humor.I. Renzoni, Eric. II. Title.
PN6231.I85R46 2010
818'.602—dc22
2010022579

This book is available at quantity discounts for bulk purchases.
For information, please call 1-800-289-0963.

DEDICATION

We dedicate this to our father, Andy, who loves a good eggplant sangweech and The Godfather.

ACKNOWLEDGMENTS

I would like to thank my brother for writing this book with me. You're a great writer, and when I thought I couldn't be funny anymore, your jokes inspired me to keep going.

Mom and Dad, thank you for your love and support. Jonny, thank you for watching countless hours of *Jersey Shore* and *The Sopranos* with me. You're an honorary Guido.

—**Andrea**

I would like to thank my sister for allowing me the opportunity to write a real book with her and for probably the first time in our lives really working together to accomplish something.

—**Eric**

CONTENTS

INTRODUCTION

What does being a Guido mean? There are a lot of ways to answer this, but here's how the current hot Guidos and Guidettes of *Jersey Shore* define it.

A Guido is [a] good lookin, smooth, well-dressed Italian.

—**The Situation**

A Guidette is somebody who knows how to club it up, takes really good care of themselves, has pretty hair, cakes on makeup, has tanned skin, wears the hottest heels. Pretty much they know how to own it and rock it.

—**Sammi**

Sure, *Jersey Shore* made being a Guido cool again (after *The Sopranos* ended), but it's more than just fake nails, tanning beds, and club hopping. Ask any Guido and he'll tell you what's *really* important to him . . . family, friends, and good food. Being a Guido is being proud of your Italian heritage. Sure, some Guidos can act like a bunch of gavones, and every now and then they need a smack in the head (which is what their Ma is for, btw). And some people take on the Guido persona even if they aren't Italian! But there's only one way to know if you're the real deal. Take a look inside this book, and at yourself, and see.

1. You Have a Tattoo of an Italian Flag Most Likely in a Place You Can't Show Your Ma

It's your eighteenth birthday. You've decided it's time to show your pride in your heritage, and you want everyone to know exactly what that is. What better way than to get the old green, white, and red tattooed on your perfectly tanned body? You could just get the basic flag on your bicep, but why be dull and simple? No, you get barbed wire stretching across your shoulder blades comprised of the three sacred colors—with stars surrounding it. You get the boot going down your stomach, with each section colored to represent the homeland you've never even visited. You get a metal cross on your entire back with the flag draped over it and the last name of some relative you heard about once that lived in a village you refer to as the "old world" written in cursive on the inside of the cross. Or if you're really ballsy, you ink that flag right on your ass. Nothing says pride like three blocks of color on your culo. Even though you may be feeding into the stereotype, and this tattoo pretty much destroys the last thing you had that was not plastered with the colors, for you it is all worth it because you are one proud Guido. Now get out on that beach and show off your new ink. Guidettes will be jumping all over your greasy, but colorful, Italian-stamped bod!

WISE GUY WISECRACKS

Tony Soprano: *What is that?*
Irina Peltsin: Chicken Soup for the Soul
Tony Soprano: *You should read Tomato Sauce for Your Ass; it's the Italian version.*

2. You Claim to Have Started the Fist Pump— And You'll Kick Ass to Prove It

It's Saturday night on the Shore. The bass is pumping at the club. Everyone's dancing and getting their drink on—the smell of hair gel and Jägermeister is in the air. Suddenly, from across the room, you spot an unfamiliar Guido pumping his fist in the air like he's trying to punch a hole in the roof. You hightail it across the dance floor, dodging hair extensions and gold chains, grab the disgraziat by his tank top shoulder straps, and yell, "I #%$!@ created the fist pump!" This scene plays itself out almost every weekend on the Shore, in one club or another, and the end result is always the same—a needless ass whupping, because in fact, no one can be credited with creating the fist pump! Cavemen may have shown excitement, anger, and probably every other emotion by pumping their fist in the air. And Arsenio Hall used a form of the fist pump on his talk show, but we all know how far that got him. . . . So just because another idiot is "beating the beat," there's no need to get all bent out of shape over it and cause a big scene. There is nothing original about pumping your fist in the air, especially as a dance move. Learning something traditional, like the foxtrot, now that would be original for a Guido.

JERSEY SHORE SOUNDBITE

It only takes 9 pounds of pressure to break a nose. —PAULY D

GUESS THAT GANGSTER #1

This famous gangster was head of his own crime family and lived to the ripe old age of ninety-seven. He hated his nickname (Joe Bananas) for good reason. His life was the subject of the book *Honor Thy Father*, by Gay Talese, and he did something no Mafia boss would have ever considered in the old days. He wrote his memoirs and was interviewed by Mike Wallace on *60 Minutes*. He told Wallace in his thick Italian accent that Al Capone was "a jolly fellow" and also defended his memoir by saying that "nobody can tell the story of [him] but [him]." Of course, like most autobiographers, he only told the story of his life that he wanted you to hear. For example, he always denied he was in the drug trade, yet his family did a brisk business in the narcotics industry. (See back of book for the answer.)

3. You Actually Own a Tanning Bed in Your Home

What better way to spend the first twenty minutes after returning home from the beach than to take a nice roast in your own personal tanning bed? You said screw it to the three-month unlimited tanning package at your local fake-'n'-bake and went right to opening up your own private shop in the basement. Never again will you show the slightest bit of Caucasian color, and people will always ask what tropical destination you just returned from. But that's just a minor inconvenience you're willing to live with if it means you can constantly resemble a California raisin. So listen up, Guidos and Guidettes: Take off that glitter thong, oil yourself from head to toe, and set that oven to bronze! You'll be smelling like a piece of roasting proscuitto in no time.

TOUGH-GUY TRIVIA

The infamous horse head scene in *The Godfather* was more horrific than you think. During rehearsals, a false horse's head was used for the bedroom scene. A real horse's head (obtained from a dog-food factory) was used for the actual shot. Woltz's scream of horror was real because no one told him a real head would be used.

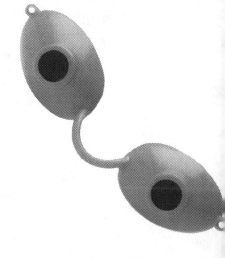

WHICH ONE OF DON CORLEONE'S SONS ARE YOU?

Vito Corelone's sons are his pride and joy (yes, even Tom Hagan, who is German-Irish). He's a big softie when it comes to his boys, and he only wants what's best for them. He spoils them, and that sometimes comes back to bite him in the ass. Which one of the Corleone boys would you be? Take the quiz to discover your Guido roots.

1. When you were a child, your favorite toy was:

A. A Barbie. You learned a lot about girls from stealing your sister's Barbie dolls. It would prove to benefit you later on in life.

B. Little green army men and a tank. You enjoyed creating strategies to surprise the enemy.

C. A book. You loved to learn new things and books offered an escape when you felt like you didn't belong.

D. Who needs toys? You could spend hours spinning around and around in a circle and still find it amusing.

2. In school, your classmates would describe you as:

A. A bully. You were always beating someone up for their milk money.

B. Quiet and reserved, yet all the girls had a secret crush on you.

C. A good student. You always had straight As.

D. Not very bright. You spent a lot of time in detention.

3. Your first girlfriend was:

A. A girl your brother had a crush on. (No woman is off-limits to you.)

B. A sweet girl you met when you came back from serving in the Army.

C. A girl your Mamma set you up with.

D. You've never had a real girlfriend, unless you count the prostitute your brothers got you for your birthday.

The best way to get your father's attention is:

A. Show him how brave you are and prove to him that you can run the family business.

B. Serve your country and come back a war hero.

C. Become a lawyer and act as an advisor to the family.

D. Drive him anywhere he wants to go and be prepared if someone tries to kill him.

5. The best thing you like about your brothers is:

A. They do anything you say since you're the oldest. And if they don't, you know how to make them.

B. They're always looking out for you since you are the youngest.

C. They come to you for advice and trust you enough to spill all of their secrets.

D. They look to you to make them laugh.

QUIZ ANSWERS

If you answered mostly As, you are Sonny Corleone. You are stubborn as a mule and expect everyone to do everything you say. You speak when you should listen and this often gets you into trouble. You're overeager and don't know how to hide your excitement when it should be hidden. You have a hard time being faithful to your wife and you might have even had an illegitimate kid. Be careful though, your hot temper might result in a hail of gunfire.

If you answered mostly Bs, you are Michael Corleone. You grew up as the shy kid that always did what his parents told him. You went to college, you joined the Army, and you found a nice girl to settle down with. You wish you could do more for the family and wish that they trusted you to do more than just answer phone calls in a crisis. You have a strong commitment to your family and will step up when the time comes. Don't try to hold all of your emotions in or it will turn you into a bitter and mean man.

If you answered mostly Cs, you are Tom Hagen. You always feel like you aren't really a part of the family. You do everything you can to prove that you belong even though this self-doubt is all in your head. You're level-headed and always think things through before you act. You are not ruled by your emotions and can keep cool in any dangerous or volatile situation. You like stability and enjoy being a family man.

If you answered mostly Ds, you are Fredo Corleone. You don't have a lot of common sense. Sometimes you have a blank look on your face that suggests you are on another planet. You're a daydreamer and a bit of a sissy. You're not strong enough to be in the family business so you're happy to act as your father's chauffeur. However, you don't act quickly when trouble arises, which leads to even more trouble. Sometimes you resent how successful your other brothers are, so when the time comes you're most likely to go behind their back to find your fortune. Lose your family's trust and you'll lose everything. Oh, and be careful in canoes.

4. You Go to the Gym for Five Hours a Day

Feel the burn, guy! You walk through that gym door and everyone knows it, unfortunately, as you look like you could be ready for the nightclub if all you did was swap out your athletic shorts for torn-up jeans. The sweatband covering the line between your forehead and precision-gelled hair shows fellow gymgoers that you mean business. The next five hours will be filled with hundreds of lightweight reps accented by the grunts and screams that will more than likely frighten anyone within thirty feet of you. In between giving winks and saying "bellissimo" to all the gym bunnies, you find the time to check yourself out in every mirror the establishment has to offer. Three protein bars and two vitamin shakes later, your time "in the zone" is over, so go flex that bulging tribal tattoo, bro . . . you've earned it.

JERSEY SHORE SOUNDBITE

You better be hittin' the gym, and if you're not hittin' the gym for like an hour or so, you know, you may have a problem. —THE SITUATION

5. You Iron Your Jeans

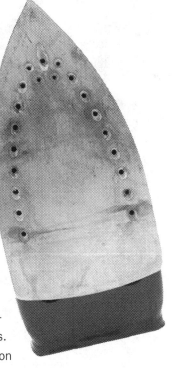

You just spent an hour ironing out every line in your loosely fitting button-up white polyester club shirt featuring black tribal art running up and down it, so why let the bottom half of your outfit go without a little attention? No one has ironed jeans since the '80s when it was deemed necessary to put creases in them—but don't let that stop you! Whip out that ironing board and get down to business. You'll be the laughingstock of the boardwalk if there's a stray wrinkle, so don't get sloppy. And don't be shy with the spray starch. That denim shouldn't move an inch while you are strutting your swagger up and down the boardwalk or getting your grind on with a little Jersey princess. Heck, while you're at it, why not get an iron-on patch of the Italian flag?

Guido Wisdom

Se niente sta andando bene, denomini la vostra nonna.

TRANSLATION: If nothing is going well, call your grandmother.

6. You Buy a Year's Supply of Hair Gel at a Time

Most people put their Costco membership to good use buying products in bulk for both the financial benefits and the convenience of not going to the store frequently. You, on the other hand, have a gold membership for one item and one item only—gallon tubs of hair gel. You go early in January, just at the start of a new year, and load three shopping carts full of one product—you don't care about the fact that other shoppers are staring and snickering. Hey, we'll see who has the last laugh when they're stuck in their homes during a blizzard with no product to keep their hair standing straight up and hard as a rock! You, being a refined Guido or Guidette, have also become very picky about the gel you use. If someone tries to hand you a bottle of Dep, you smack him in the face. This isn't amateur hour. Get the good stuff or fuhgeddaboudit!

JERSEY SHORE SOUNDBITE

There's no way I'm going to Jersey without my hair gel. Can't leave without my gel.—PAULY D

7. You Hold a Cigar in Your Mouth Even If It's Not Lit

The stogie—arguably the ultimate accessory for any real Guido—is a permanent fixture in your hand, but only when you are trying to portray that certain sophisticated look. It is not like you would ever actually smoke it, but in a Guido's world it is not necessary for it to be lit because it's all for show. You are convinced it looks cool to have one just hanging out of your mouth. You are not concerned with getting quality cigars from Cuba or the Dominican Republic, or even having a humidor to hold them. You will buy any random pack at the gas station, even the cheap ones with fake wooden tips, right before you head out with your boys. No matter how hard you try though, you are never going to look as cool as Tony Soprano does when he blows a thick cloud of smoke out of his mouth in an expensive suit. Keep on walking around with an unlit cigar in your mouth though, and some out-of-state tourist to the Jersey area might think you are a true-life gangster!

WISE GUY WISECRACKS
Q. *How is the Italian version of Christmas different?*
A. *One Mary, one Jesus, and thirty-two wise guys.*

8. You're Still Having Debates over Which Was Better, *The Godfather* or *The Godfather: Part II*

Pacino and DeNiro—two of the greatest Italian-American actors—were involved in these pieces of cinematic genius (*The Godfather: Part III* doesn't count, but it was a piece of something alright), but that was nearly forty years ago! It's time to move on. These films are so important to you, you don't even refer to them as *The Godfather* or *The Godfather: Part II*, they're just "one" and "two" and your friends know exactly what you're talking about. Sure, you could go on and on about which scene takes the cake: Michael gunning down McCluskey and Sollozzo at Louis's Restaurant in the Bronx (c'mon, you know you still scream "Drop the gun!" even though you've seen it fifty times) or when Vito goes home to Sicily to take sweet revenge at Don Ciccio's villa. You might even argue that even though James Caan isn't Italian, he still makes one hell of a gangster. This may be one of the only times in film history that you can say a sequel was better than the original, but let's face it, you'll always find some chooch that will go round twelve with you to make a final determination.

> **PAISANO Says**
>
> **Priest:** Tony prefers two to one?
> **Carmela Soprano:** Ya, he likes it when Vito goes back to Sicily. In three, it was like . . . what happened??

TOUGH-GUY TRIVIA

There had been talk of a fourth Godfather film, but it never actually happened. Just as *The Godfather: Part II* told the parallel stories of the young Don Corleone and son Michael, the fourth film would have explored the lives of the young Sonny Corleone (played by Leonardo DiCaprio) and his illegitimate son, Vincent.

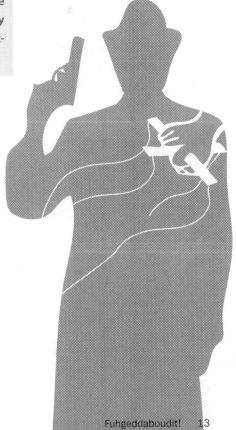

9. You'll Get a Sausage and Peppers on the Boardwalk Even If You Just Ate

You know there is always room for a big sausage and peppers torpedo, guy! Sure, you may have just polished off a dish of your mother's veal scallopini, but now you are headed down to the boardwalk and that aroma no Guido can resist has found its way up your flaring nostrils. Your mouth starts to salivate, and, in typical fashion, you yell your order to the guy at the stand from about twenty yards out so that he knows you're coming. Like you always say, "Nothing washes down a big plate of mom-made pasta like a sausage and peppers from the boardwalk." As long as the guy working the stand isn't new, he should just need to see (or hear) you approaching and, since he knows your order by heart, it is good to go by the time you get there. You pretty much consider the sausage-and-pepper guy a close friend at this point. Hell, why not get one for your Guidette while you are at it? This way, you can both stink like a greasy sausage.

GUESS THAT GANGSTER #2

This man was the son of a gangster who wanted him to follow in his criminal footsteps, something that almost never happened in Mafia machinations. This prompted what was whimsically known as "the Banana War." It was a protracted mob war that left many dead. Like his father, he also went public with his life story late in his life. He was interviewed on A&E's *Biography* about his famous father. (See back of the book for the answer.)

WHICH *JERSEY SHORE* GUIDO ARE YOU?

You've worshipped them for months. You can't stop saying "GTL," and you've given yourself a nickname. Now find out which *Jersey Shore* Guido you'd play on the show.

1. At the end of a long night of club hopping and trying to pick up chicks, you are:

A. Checking to make sure the temp is hot enough in the hot tub so you can entertain some honeys

B. Making out with your boss's chick, even though she's twenty years older than you

C. Taking a grenade for the team so your boy can get some play

D. In bed actually having sex

2. When you grow up, you are mostly likely to become:

A. A fitness instructor that doesn't do much but check himself out in the mirror

B. A lawyer or teacher

C. A bald DJ (too much hair gel for thirty years made it fall out)

D. A fugitive because you didn't show up for your assault sentence

3. If someone asked you if you would ever get married, you'd say:

A. "As soon as the right one comes along."

B. "My Ma will kill me if I don't have kids soon, so probably in the next five years."

C. "How can I get married when all I find are stalkers?"

D. "I'm practically married as it is."

4. **Your favorite thing to eat after a night of drinking is:**

A. A protein shake

B. My mom's baked ziti

C. A slice and a Coke

D. A couple pieces of white bread and some juice

5. **A typical Saturday night for you is:**

A. Spending my time collecting phone numbers from as many girls as possible and inviting a girl and all of her friends back to the house to party, then sleeping alone.

B. Studying for the LSATs before heading to the club where I will catch pinkeye because I've danced with a dirty girl.

C. Flirting with every girl in the club then wondering why they follow me home when they weren't invited and won't stop calling me.

D. Showing of my battle skills at the club, punching some guy in the face because he won't stop running his mouth, then spending the next three hours crying with my girlfriend because I scare her when I'm angry.

QUIZ ANSWERS

If you answered mostly As, you are Mike "The Situation." You have more confidence than anyone in the world, but most of the time it's all an act. When you get hurt, you don't hide your feelings well. For a guy that acts like a player all the time, you do have the potential to fall in love. Show the girls who you really are, not a persona to project.

If you answered mostly Bs, you are Vinnie. You're a Mamma's boy at heart. You don't like being compared to the stereotypical Guido, even though you exhibit some of those traits every now and then. You're quick to tell people you finished college so they don't think you're just another stunad. Nothing makes you happier than being with your family. Out of all of your friends, you'll probably get married first.

If you answered mostly Cs, you are Pauly D. You're a pretty boy all the way that can charm the pants off the ladies. It usually works, too, until they become obsessed with you. You've had to fight off the honeys plenty of times, especially in your line of work. Your main goal in life is to have fun and not get too serious. You're close to your boys, and your favorite thing to do on the weekend is GTL (gym, tan, and laundry, baby!)

If you answered mostly Ds, you are Ronnie. In general, you're a sweet guy. Girls immediately see the soft side of you and it reels them in. However, you do have a violent temper that can get out of control if provoked. Let the girl you're with know this up front so she's not surprised when you get in a fight at the bar. You'll do anything to protect your friends, even if that means punching someone else in the mouth. Try to take a few deep breaths before going berserk.

10. You Have No Problem with Stealing Someone's Guido or Guidette at the Club

When you are on a mission to score, nothing is going to stand in your way—not even the fact that the person in question is already grinding up against some sweaty guy or girl. You see them across the room and your blood starts flowing. The lights are in strobe mode so it is difficult to tell what you are looking at exactly—but hey, does it really matter? Once you have set your tractor beam on the target, there is no turning back. You take one last shot of cheap vodka and subtly fist-pump your way over to where they are grinding, er, dancing. Without so much as an introduction, you weasel your way in between them and give the girl that self-proclaimed "infamous" eye contact. Now you know that in no time you'll be firing up the hot tub and sealing the deal back at your Shore house. She is so wasted, she doesn't even know who she is dancing with at this point, and the person she was with is slow to figure out what the hell happened. You get a tap on the shoulder and dodge a left hook while coming in with the uppercut. One hit and he is out for the count, while you are being thrown out by bouncers. Luckily, you still have the object of your affection's arm in your hand so she's coming with you. You will risk a rumble or two to get what you want—let's just hope honey is worth it.

JERSEY SHORE SOUNDBITE

Your number one mission is to go out and find the hottest Guido and take him home. —SAMMI

11. You Made a Trip to Pizzaland Because You Saw It on *The Sopranos'* Opening Credits

For six years you watched Tony drive by the now-famous pizzeria every day on his way home, so naturally you decide it would be a great idea to make a road trip. This is probably the first time anyone has ever traveled to get a piece of pizza. Pay no attention to the fact that it is probably the same greasy slice you can get from any one of the ten pizza dives down the street, but if it is good enough for Tony Soprano, it is good enough for you. You will do anything to be a part of the Soprano crew, so if that means driving for hours, or even days, so be it! Pizzaland is located at 260 Belleville Turnpike in North Arlington, New Jersey, so turn on the GPS, pack some cannolis for the road, and get ready to chow down. If you have not already been there, now there is no excuse. Or you could go all out and splurge on one of those special Soprano tours they give and stop at all the important landmarks—including good ol' Pizzaland. Be sure to pick up a T-shirt so you can brag to your buds back home who wouldn't make the drive with you. If getting there in person is out of the question, fear not. Pizzaland now ships either 14-inch or 9-inch pies anywhere in the United States. You will be snacking like your favorite wise guys in no time!

Guido Wisdom
Nella vita, chi non risica non rosica.
TRANSLATION: In life, who risks nothing, gains nothing.

12. You Named Your Dog after an Italian Delicacy

You love your pooch more than anything in the world. He is your best friend, your pride and joy. He is so cute that people have asked you out on a date just so you would take your baby along. You would do absolutely anything for him in return. When you first got him, you thought long and hard about which name would be appropriate. If you are a real Guido, this should have been a piece of ricotta pie. The only way to go is to name him after an Italian delicacy, like "Meatball," "Cannoli," or "Pannetone." Guidos have no problem owning tiny dogs. And Guidettes can fit their pooch in their purse, so calling him "Meatball" is just too cute for words. For larger, more butch dogs, you will want to go with something strong, like "Rigatoni" or "Manicotti." Remember though that only certain Italian foods will work. Calling a dog "Broccoli Rabe" or "Veal Parmesan" just isn't going to fly. Pick the right dish and you have a winning moniker that will let your best friend stand out in a crowd.

GUIDO HOT SPOTS

In season 5 of *The Sopranos*, the racetrack they go to is actually Riverhead Raceway in Riverhead, Long Island.

13. You Think the Perfect Meal Is a Slice and a Coke

Despite having access to the most amazing Italian food all the time at your Ma's house, sometimes you have to stick with the simple classics. For breakfast, lunch, or dinner, the best Guido meal is a slice and a Coke. Just one bite takes you back to the good old days of hanging out at the mall and scamming on the little thirteen-year-old honeys at the food court. And we are not talking deep-dish here. If your crust is more than an inch thick, you are gettin' a beatin'. New York style is the only way to go. You also do not go crazy with the toppings. You have never ordered a meat-lovers pizza or a Hawaiian pizza. For you, it is all about the classics—plain cheese, Margherita, or pepperoni. Sprinkle some Parm cheese and maybe some crushed red pepper flakes and you are on your way to a dynamite snack. Your local pizzeria is like your second home. You may have even worked there as a kid. There is nothing like going to the same pizzeria you've been visiting since you were five and wolfing down a slice before heading out to work or on your way home from the club. It is the perfect way to soak up a belly full of booze. Nothing goes better with a slice than a Coke. It's the ultimate comfort food, and you cannot wait until you have kids so you can introduce them to the best food group going.

Guido Wisdom

A correre e cagare ci si immerda i garretti.

TRANSLATION: By running and defecating at the same time, you'll get crap on your heels.

14. Your Nonnie Has Looked Elderly Since She Turned Fifty

God bless your Nonnie! You cannot remember when she didn't look like she was eighty years old. It's like one day she woke up and she shrunk a whole twelve inches and her hair turned completely white. As soon as she had her last child, she donned a black dress and has not taken it off for the last thirty or forty years. Her hair has also been in a bun for that long. Have you ever seen her with her hair down? I didn't think so. She ties a black scarf around her head as soon as she steps out of the house. It is

on when she goes to the local baker every day for fresh bread and on Sunday morning on her way to Mass. She is the cutest thing you have ever seen. She does not leave the kitchen unless it is to take trays of ziti to the table or pour you another glass of Fresca. She begs you to "Mangia, mangia," but you have never actually seen her eat. Your Nonnie will be around forever. It's the olive oil she rubs on her face every night that keeps her so well-preserved. So make your Nonnie proud and go visit every now and then. You are bound to get a meal out of it and some leftovers to take home.

15. You Still Think It's Cool to Talk Like Tony Montana

In 1983, Scarface came out. In 1983, it was epic. In 1983, Tony Montana was the coolest. But c'mon, after nearly thirty years, isn't it time to let the voice go? We know you own each "special" edition that has come out on DVD. We know you have the movie poster hanging in the basement den of your parent's house. Please stop trying to sound like Tony. You are doing him and everything he stands for a disservice. No, we will not say hello to your little friend . . . idiot. It is fine if you want to idolize these great characters—the Tony Sopranos, the Sonnys, the Michael Corleones—but for all of our sake, leave the voices and the quotations to the pros.

> **" PAISANO Says**
>
> This ain't negotiation time. This is Scarface, final scene, fuckin' bazookas under each arm, say hello to my little friend! —**Christopher Moltisanti, The Sopranos** "

GUIDE TO GUIDO LANGUAGE	
WORD	MEANING
Agita	heartburn/acid indigestion
Batz	crazy
Butan	whore
Cafone/gavone	a peasant or someone beneath you in class
Chooch	blockhead
Disgraziat	a disgrace
Facia bruta	ugly face

GUIDE TO GUIDO LANGUAGE

Gabagool	capicola ham
Gabbadotz	hardheaded
Googootz	a term of endearment/slang for zucchini
Goombah	a fellow Guido or wannabe Mafioso
Goomah	girlfriend or mistress
Gravy	tomato sauce
Grenade	an unattractive girl that hangs out with hot girls
GTL	gym, tanning, and laundry
Madonn'	holy smoke/holy shit
Manicott	manicotti
Mezza fanook	half sissy/slang for homosexual
Mortadella	loser
Moozarell	mozzerella
Musciata	mushy
Oogatz	like hell
Paisano	literally means your cousin or countryman
Proshoot	proscuitto
Rigott	ricotta cheese
Schifosa	a very ugly woman
Sfatcheem	pain in the ass
Statazit	shut up
Staten Island tuxedo	a velour track suit
Stugots	testicles, or often used to call someone an asshole
Stunad	an idiot or lightheaded person
Vafanculo	the F word
Va fa nabola	go to hell

16. You Practice Your Battle Skills in the Mirror Before Going to the Club

If you want to show you have any moves at all at the club, you need to practice. You stand in front of your floor-length mirror with no clothes on except for a baseball cap, turn some house music on, and start dancing away. After about an hour, your Ma tells you to turn down the devil music. You're ready anyway. No one is going to get in your way tonight. When it comes to battling, you think you're the best. You and some other dude face to face, trying to see who can come up with the sickest move. You're both gyrating, throwing arms and legs anywhere they will go, looking like a couple of freaks. Meanwhile, your boys are behind you urging you to kick this guy's ass and claim the title of Best Battler on the Block. The ladies are flocking around you, cups in hand, giggling and whispering to their girlfriends "If he can move like that on the dance floor . . . ." Little do they know, once you're done here, you're probably done for the night. Battling takes a lot of energy. It's a good thing you whipped up that protein shake before heading out. So take another shot and get this over with. Don't hurt yourself, now.

Guido Wisdom
Una buona mamma vale cento maestre.
TRANSLATION: A good mother is worth a hundred teachers.

WHICH *JERSEY SHORE* GUIDETTE ARE YOU?

You love the way these girls dress, talk, and act. You're dying to have the Snooki Poof and make your own clothes like J-WOWW. Take the quiz below to find out which *Jersey Shore* Guidette you would play on the show.

1. At the end of a long night of club hopping and trying to pick up juiceheads, you are:

A. Calling your boyfriend to reassure him that you didn't cheat on him (even though you did)

B. Hooking up with your steady boyfriend in the guest bedroom

C. Whining about not finding anyone to make out with at the club

D. Messing up your roommates' game (if you aren't getting any, no one can!)

2. When you grow up, you are mostly likely to become:

A. A has-been "fashion designer" or a stripper turned porn star

B. A divorcée who got all her husband's money in the divorce

C. A mom with ten Guido kids who lives in Jersey

D. Unemployed, because you can never make it into work so you constantly get fired

3. If someone asked you if you would ever get married, you'd say:

A. "If my husband will let me have an open relationship."

B. "If I can learn how to trust the man I'm with."

C. "If I can find a guy that really likes me for me."

D. "If I can find a guy that will put up with all of my bullshit."

Your favorite thing to eat after a night of drinking is:
A. Ham and water

B. Ripped up pieces of white bread

C. Pickles

D. You're too busy yelling at your roommates to eat

 A typical Saturday night for you is:
A. Creating my outfit from scratch, finding a guy to hook up with, and ripping his head off

B. Watching my boyfriend dance with other girls at the club, then walking home by myself to cry in my pillow

C. Doing backflips on the floor of the club and trying to get a boy to kiss me or punch me in the mouth

D. Spying on my roommates who are trying to hook up in the hot tub

QUIZ ANSWERS

If you answered mostly As, you are J-WOWW. You've said it yourself: you're a rough girl who treats guys like pieces of meat. But you still like to have a boyfriend around. Even if that means you cheat on him. You love your body and have no shame when it comes to putting an outfit together for the club. You'll expose all your naughty bits to attract some attention. If another Guidette gets in your face, you'll punch her lights out and are proud of it. You don't take any shit from anyone.

If you answered mostly Bs, you are Sammi. You're a bit of a two-face. You're a sweetheart one second, and a hormonal mess the next. You don't trust anyone, especially the guys you date. You have some self-esteem issues you need to work on if you plan on having a steady man in your life. Accusing them of cheating every five seconds isn't going to fly; Especially if you have no problem bouncing from one guy to the next. Deep down you want to settle down and have a family, but you have a long way to go.

If you answered mostly Cs, you are Snooki. You are the life of the party and don't know what to do if you're not the center of attention. You live in your own little world, and anyone who's around to witness it always has a good laugh. You have a bubbly personality and are nice to everyone you meet, until they do something to piss you off. You might not be the brightest bulb, but you make up for it with your charm, even if some people find you annoying every now and then.

If you answered mostly Ds, you are Angelina. You love to start a fight. Whether it's over strange girls in the hot tub, your boyfriend not calling you back, or even another girl giving you a strange look, you have no problem raising your voice to let everyone know you are pissed off. You like to be in everyone's business but don't want anyone to question anything you do. You have a hard time holding down a job because you don't deal well with authority. You're in charge of whatever you do, not anyone else.

17. You've "Beat a Bitch Down"

You're shaking your thang at the club, sipping on a rum and coke, when all of a sudden you see a group of Guidettes looking at you, whispering and making faces. You continue to do your thing while alerting your girls to the situation. There might be a rumble brewing and you need all hands on deck. After a few insults are thrown back and forth, things start to heat up. All it takes is one skanky trashbag sitting at the bar calling you fat and you're taking out your gold hoop earrings and passing your fake Fendi to your friend faster than you can say "vafanculo!" The rules are simple: When it comes to "beating a bitch down," whoever grabs the first fistful of hair will win. As soon as you feel you have a good hold, don't let go unless your life depends on it. You can swing that bitch around the room if you have to. No one talks trash about you and leaves without a black eye. However, unless you know what you're doing, don't try to throw punches. You're just going to break your hand and ruin your $30 acrylic tips. Just go for the hair and wait for the bouncers. If all else fails, tell your juicehead that her juicehead was hitting on you and let the men go at it as you scream and take swings from the background.

JERSEY SHORE SOUNDBITE

I was gonna try to uppercut her, but at that point I had too many bouncers wrapped around me. I just wish for like three more seconds. I woulda done justice. —J-WOWW

18. You Own More Than Two Ed Hardy Shirts

Loud colors, ridiculous designs, and outrageous prices—you love it all when it comes to Ed Hardy! What better way to show that you are top peacock than to wear a skin-tight T-shirt with sparkling gold skulls and rainbow lettering? Gaudy does not begin to describe the abomination you have on. You balanced your glowing skull-laden tee with a pair of prefaded and pretorn dark blue jeans, which features a dragon running from the back pockets all the way down to the ankles—but you don't stop there. Your banana yellow hat features the words "love," "believe," and "kill," and thirty-two snakes, seventeen tiger faces, and eight hearts can be counted on your sick gear. This is all for nought though, because no one can look at you directly due to the sunlight reflecting off the cross on your chain, the diamonds in your Movado, and the studs on your belt. But don't worry, if anyone wants to know what you look like they can simply glance over at one of your "crew" members and see the same exact outfit...in different colors, of course.

> **TOUGH-GUY TRIVIA**
>
> Tony Soprano was originally going to be called Tommy Soprano.

19. You Consider Your Manicurist One of Your Best Friends

Is her name Sharlene, Debbie, or Heather? Either way, you have known her since you were thirteen when your mom brought you in for your first mani. She has seen you through ups and downs, ins and outs. She knows everything about you because this is not just a time to get your nails done—it is a time to spill your guts. She knows the name of every boyfriend you have had since you were a kid and how much of a jerk each one of them was. She knows your hopes and your fears. When you're having a rough day, she knows exactly how to make you feel better. The smell of cigarette that comes off her breath when she is leaning over you brings a comforting wave of familiarity that's usually reserved for family members. At the holidays, she can do up your nails with spiders, Christmas trees, and even Easter eggs! And on a special occasion, she will hook you up with a real treat—gold glitter and fake Swarovski crystals on your three-inch acrylics. Most importantly, she knows how to add black tips to a French manicure, à la Jersey Shore's J-WOWW. What comforts you the most is the fact that she has not left your favorite nail salon in twenty years. It gives you a feeling of calm inside to know that with all the craziness in the world, Sharlene, or Debbie, or Heather will always be there.

GUIDO HOT SPOTS

Want your nails to look just like Adriana's in *The Sopranos*? Head to Finger Fitness Salon in Cliffside Park, New Jersey, and ask for Maria Salandra. She was often the stylist for Adriana. She can add leopard spots and animal patterns or designer logos and fake jewels.

20. You Won't Leave the House Without Your Hair Extensions

Forget taking care of your real hair. You've bleached it so many times, it is practically falling out. There is only one solution: buy some fake hair. You think the person that invented fake hair is a genius, and you would not be caught DEAD without your extensions. God forbid someone realizes you do not actually have the long, luxurious locks that you are seen with at the club every night. It takes a lot to look that good (like a couple hundred dollars . . . or twenty bucks online if you are really desperate). Chances are, after three or four rum and diet cokes at the club, you are so sloppy you do not notice that you have started to pull them out of your head right there on the dance floor. It's cool; they just clip on, right? If anyone questions it, simply blame it on some rare disease that you got drinking the tap water in Jersey.

JERSEY SHORE SOUNDBITE

That's kind of a turn off, when a girl acts sloppy. —PAULY D

GUESS THAT GANGSTER #3

He is perhaps the most famous gangster in the long and bloody history of the Mafia. He got his start on the mean streets of New York City but eventually ventured out to the windy city of Chicago. There he became the Kingpin of Crime during the Roaring Twenties. His battle with Treasury agent Eliot Ness and his band of Untouchables has become the stuff of American legend and the subject of both TV and big-screen renditions. He was a ruthless killer who personally killed many men and ordered the deaths of many more, but what finally brought him down was a conviction and jail sentence for income tax evasion. (See back of the book for the answer.)

21. Your Favorite Thing to Do on a Saturday Morning Is Get a Pedicure and You're a Guy

A nice warm soak in a scented tub, a refreshing sea salt scrub, and an hour of cuticle-cutting bliss—a real man takes care of his feet. All those nights of battling on the dance floor, running down the street after some stunad who called your mother a whore, and hours at the gym in germ-infested locker rooms can do a number on your little piggies. And let's not even talk about the exfoliating that needs to be done after baking in the tanning bed. For a man that likes to wear his Adidas sandals year round (with or without socks), you know the importance of a good pedicure

once a week. You've thought about getting a gift certificate for your goomah, but you just cannot bring yourself to lose all the potential tail that works at the salon by showing them you have a woman. So get the boys together and head out to the nail salon. If you are lucky, the pedicurist will think you are a stud and will give you her number.

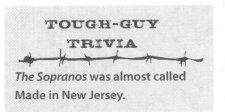

TOUGH-GUY TRIVIA

The Sopranos was almost called Made in New Jersey.

22. You Smoke Menthol Lite Cigarettes but Only when You're Partying

Being a true Guido, you prefer to smoke a stogie (a Cuban at that, so everyone knows you're above the law), but if one isn't available your next choice to show how much of a man you are is to spark up a menthol lite cigarette. With a cigarette in one hand and a Long Island Ice Tea in the other, the cool feel of menthol burning your lungs hits the spot and makes you smell awesome by the end of the night. You had your first butt at age twelve in your friend Stevie's tree house while looking at girly magazines, and you've been hooked ever since. You were never as cool as you were at twelve years old. Now, you aren't a two-pack-a-day type of smoker; you just like to light up when the beat is pumping and the drinks are flowing. And chances are if you forgot to pick some up before heading out, everyone else in the club will be able to hook you up.

Ladies, while you wouldn't be caught dead smoking a smelly cigar, you agree that a thick cloud of menthol smoke at the club is a powerful aphrodisiac. Just remember not to light up while you are spraying more hair spray to your already rock hard 'do. That is just an accident waiting to happen. You will have to buy more hair extensions than you already have. So take a puff and send out the vibe. Some hottie is bound to come a runnin'.

HOW TO SPOT A GUIDO MAMMA

1. She never minds her own business. She feels it is her right after giving birth to you to know the innermost secrets of your life.

2. She turns dinner into a production. She spends hours in the kitchen meticulously slicing and dicing to create a masterpiece for the palette, and everything is so fabulous there are never any leftovers. "For my son, his favorite lasagna; for my husband, his favorite sausage and peppers; and for me . . . well, I didn't have time so I'll just sit here and enjoy watching you two eat."

3. She makes Tony Soprano look like a softie. She doesn't consider it being vindictive—rather an eye for an eye, a tooth for a tooth. She's like the grandmother in Moonstruck who stood next to Cher's character as a plane carrying Cher's fiancé took off, and then the sweet-looking, little old Italian grandmother (dressed head-to-toe in black) announced that her sister was on the same plane and that she put a curse on it so it would crash. To this mama, it's all in day's work.

4. She cannot imagine a life without grandchildren. She has been waiting for this day since her own child was born. If you open her top drawer, you will see a stash of booties, hats, and blankets that she has been knitting over the years. Look even closer and you will see that there are names on the items. You didn't think that these grandchildren wouldn't be named after her? Think again.

5. She has a knack for failing to remember things that definitely happened. "I never said that" or "That didn't happen" are her two favorite phrases.

6. She believes in God, the Catholic Church, and good china, not necessarily in that order. Her home is spotless and orderly, with a cross in every bedroom and statues of David and the Pietà in the

cabinet that also displays every piece of her wedding china. She's fond of saying, "Don't sit on the furniture in the living room. It's for guests."

7. She doesn't drive and relies on her husband and son to take her to church and the grocery store. She likes to get there early so she can have her pick of the good pews and good produce.

8. She redefines the blowout when it comes to holidays—they are so elaborate they resemble a Broadway show. Every inch of the house is decorated so brightly the house could be seen from space. Twelve courses of food are served on fine linens and good china. At some point, she will smile and say, "Now I can die in peace. My whole family is here, and we are together. May God bless us and watch over us."

23. You Know What It Means to Beat the Beat

The bass is thumping. The volume is slowly rising. All over the dance floor there are small groups of Italian men and women shaking and hopping around. You are down on the ground in a circle of your friends, pounding the floor with your fist. As the tempo increases, you slowly move up, yet that fist does not stop pumping. Slowly rising as the music reaches its crescendo, your fist is flying in the air with abandon. You're having your own personal battle as you beat that beat. You've reached fist-pumping nirvana. You are one with the beat. There is nothing you like better than dancing your stress away with your friends. You trade signature moves and are desperate to create the hottest new dance craze. For now, you are still beating the beat like the best of them. Someday your arm will have no feeling from all the fist pumping you do. But you look cool doing it, so who cares?

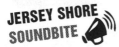

JERSEY SHORE SOUNDBITE

We're beatin' up the beat, that's what we say when we're doing our fist pump. First, we start off by banging the ground. We're banging it as the beat builds 'cause that beat's hittin' us so we're fightin' back. It's like we beat up that beat. —**PAULY D**

24. You Obsessively Clean Your Sneakers

Just think—if you ever decide to move out of your parent's basement and get a job, you could be one heck of a shoe polisher! Those white kicks of yours are blinding, and if you're out on the scene and the smallest speck of dirt gets on them, you're on it like a Guidette on a juicehead. God help the punk that scuffs up your pair of Adidas's, because after you run to the bathroom, pull out your emergency shoe shine kit, and get that scuff out, that fool is in for an old-school Italian beatdown at the hands of you and your crew! But don't go stomping on him, because you might get blood on your shoes! If a bat is handy, feel free to use that—just like the guys you watch in the movies. Then just for show, maybe one of you can throw him into the trunk of the car, but make sure to take him out before you return it to your parents.

❝PAISANO Says

Go home and get your shine box.

—**Billy Batts,** *Goodfellas* ❞

TOUGH-GUY
TRIVIA

Many mob buffs argue over exactly who *The Godfather* was modeled after. Some speculate that Carlo Gambino was the model for Don Corleone, while others point to Sam DeCavalcante, Vito Genovese, or Joe Bonanno.

25. There Are Always Trays of Your Mom's Lasagna in the Fridge and Freezer

Nobody makes lasagna like your Mamma . . . NOBODY! She even has her own special recipe that distinguishes it from anyone else's lasagna. You could pick hers out of a lineup if you had to. How can you be expected to survive if you are away from home? You need to plan in advance. You go down to the Shore for the summer—leaving behind the comforts of the basement you have grown to love, the family you spend every Sunday evening with, and the bathroom mirror you have taken so many MySpace pictures in—but the home cooking you grew up on and still live for is one comfort you can't leave behind. So you've got ten-pound tin foil pans of lasagna with a tight layer of aluminum foil making the trip with you, strapped into the passenger seat by a seat belt. You have also got one hand holding onto it for dear life, just like a mother protecting her child in the front seat. You would think it was a tin foil pan full of gold by the way you are protecting it. As soon as you get to the Shore house, one tray gets placed into the fridge for easy access, such as when you get home from the club at the early morning hours, and the other gets put right into the freezer as emergency backup, like when you have run out of the first pan and thoughts of missing your basement back home are really getting to you. F%@#in' love ya, Ma!

Guido Wisdom
A chi dai il dito si prende anche il braccio.
LITERAL TRANSLATION: Give them a finger and they'll take an arm.

26. You Live in Your Parents' Basement Even Though You Graduated Ten Years Ago

You were eighteen when you made the big move from the bedroom of your childhood in that little raised ranch in Jersey . . . to the basement of your adulthood in that little raised ranch in Jersey. You graduated high school and needed more freedom and privacy, so you took over the basement den and made it your own little haven. Now, at twenty-eight, not much has changed for you or your living quarters. Sure, you swapped out that *21 Jump Street* poster for a *Sopranos* one, but who are we kidding when it comes to you and possibly moving out from under your parent's roof? If you are hitting the clubs well into your thirties, why not live with your parents for the same amount of time? All the neighborhood boys are still in the neighborhood with you, living out their own fantasies from their own basements up and down the street. Everything is familiar and comfortable, so why bother growing up and getting a real job in the real world? Plus, if any little Guidette asks—you are a senior in college and you are home on break.

GUIDO HOT SPOTS

The Sopranos live at the fictional 633 Stag Trail Road, North Caldwell, New Jersey. The house used in exterior shots is actually located at 14 Aspen Drive in North Caldwell.

ATTENTION, GUIDETTES: IS YOUR STUD A MAMMONE?

Many proud Guidos are also proud to be mammoni or "mamma's boys," that is, fully grown men who gleefully remain tied to—dependent upon—their mothers. Italian mothers love to pamper and spoil their boys, so much so that they often live at home long after finding good, stable jobs until a wife intervenes. And their doting mothers spoil them by providing their favorite meals, crisply ironed shirts, and a spotless abode. To all the Guidettes out there, mammoni can be handsome, sexy, rich, chic, and everything you long to have, but if you cannot accept that Mamma Mia comes first, the romance may never get off the ground. To find out, choose all that apply to your guy.

A. He wears perfectly pressed shirts and pants yet doesn't spend a dime on dry-cleaning.

B. His refrigerator is always chock full of homemade pasta, yet he doesn't own a single pan.

C. His apartment is immaculate, yet he has neither a broom nor a housekeeper.

D. His socks and underwear are spotless and always folded neatly.

E. He always, always promptly takes his mother's calls.

F. All of the above

QUIZ ANSWERS

Answer: Yep, it's F—definitely all of the above, and a thousand other clues. Warning: The Mamma love can look attractive in the beginning, but later on, when it becomes a ménage à trois (and we don't mean a sexual romp), mamma will steamroll over anyone that gets between her and her son—and that means you, sister.

27. You Invite Your Mom Over Because You Know She'll Clean Your Apartment

You finally made it out of the folks' place and into your own bachelor pad . . . a place where you and the boys can kick back, watch UFC with your Tapout shirts on while you scream at the television, high-five each other, and drink Heineken until the wee hours of the morning. Eventually you might even have a few select Guidettes come by and check out the place, but before that can happen you better have Mamma stop by and clean the place up! You may have flown from the nest, but baby bird is still under Mamma bird's wing—and he always will be. One phone call and she's over in a heartbeat with a pan of eggplant Parmesan, a bottle of Fresca, and a pack of new white tank tops for you. Being a Mamma's boy just comes with the Guido territory . . . and you couldn't be happier about it.

GUIDO HOT SPOTS

The Bada Bing strip club is actually a go-go bar in Lodi, New Jersey, called Satin Dolls.

YOUR LAST NAME IS PROBABLY . . .

If you're a real Guido, your last name is probably one of the following. Here are the twenty most common Italian last names.

ROSSI	BRUNO
RUSSO	GALLO
FERRARI	CONTI
ESPOSITO	DE LUCA
BIANCHI	COSTA
ROMANO	GIORDANO
COLOMBO	MANCINI
RICCI	RIZZO
MARINO	LOMBARDI
GRECO	MORETTI

28. You Spend a Half-Hour Creating the Perfect Blowout

There is no excuse for walking out of the house without the blowout. Before you are ready for prime time, you need to make sure you are in tip-top shape. Those pencil-thin sideburns have been shaved down in the shape of an L, the sides and back of your hairline are all taped up, and the cut is gradient from low all the way up to a near afro on top. The fresh cut is in place, and now it is time to work your magic in the mirror. With both hands filled with healthy globs of hair gel, it is now all about pulling that hair as high up and far away from your scalp as humanly possible. Your blow dryer is your best friend. It has been with you since the beginning as you created your signature hairdo. You could never have achieved greatness without it. If it breaks down, you will buy a new one but hold on to the old one as a keepsake. You have a closet full of broken blow dryers. You owe it your life. If you can go from being 5'8" to 6'4" in just a half-hour, you are a certified Guido with a gift.

JERSEY SHORE SOUNDBITE

My hair's windproof, waterproof, soccerproof, motocycleproof. I'm not sure if my hair's bulletproof, I'm not willin' to try that.
—PAULY D

29. You Buy Jeans with Holes Already in Them

As you pull up to Macy's in the BMW your parents bought you for your sixteenth birthday, you know you have to find that perfect pair of designer jeans for the club tonight. You could care less that you are about to spend well over $100 for about $3 worth of fabric that was thrown together in a sweatshop. You know exactly what you are looking for: They have to be tight, they have to look bleached, and they have to be filled with holes. As long as you can clip your cell onto the side of them and you look like every other Guido with basically the same pair on in the club, they are good to go. Today looks like your lucky day, too, because it seems they are having a clearance on a pair with some skulls woven onto the back pockets! The goombah gods must be looking down on you.

TOUGH-GUY
TRIVIA

According to *Maxim* magazine, Joe Pesci wrote and directed the "You think I'm funny?" scene in *Goodfellas* at Martin Scorsese's request.

30. The Night Doesn't End until You've Hooked Up in the Hot Tub

All those hours of trying to lure some hottie you've had your eye on all night for a little innocent soak better pay off with some nookie in the tub of love. Something about the smell of chlorine just screams sex, and you might get away without having to wrap your salami (there is no way your boys can live in 101 degrees, right?), but that is a chance you are willing to take for someone you won't see ever again. But hittin' it in the tub is not as easy as you might think. You've got to have all the smooth moves. You keep a bottle of bath bubbles to add to the ambience and to make the shy girls more comfortable. You also keep a bottle of body oil nearby in case someone needs a massage. If you feel you need to pull out the big guns to land that perfect broad, you have a box of rubber duckies you're ready to throw in. If things are going to get real hot and heavy, you've got that little tube of oil-based lube ready to go. Face it. You just need to get your rocks off so you can go to sleep, so fire the whirlpool jets, remove the thong, and get down to business. HOWEVER, do not forget to give the tub a scrubbing before inviting the next girl in—that is just classless.

A GUIDO MADE THAT?

We're not all mortadellas. Some of the greatest inventors were Italian. Bet you didn't know Guidos were responsible for the awesome items below:

- **The barometer**—also called "Torricelli's tube," this device was invented by Evangelista Torricelli
- **Carbon paper**—invented in 1806 by Pellegrino Turri of Italy

- **Cursive handwriting**—thank Aldus Manutius for having to learn this useless skill in elementary school
- **The electric battery**—Allessandro Volta invented this in 1800
- **The Jacuzzi**—leave it to a Guido to invent this wonder; in 1968, Roy Jacuzzi invented the best place to hook up
- **Liposuction**—if you ever need fat sucked out of you, thank Dr. Giorgio Fischer for inventing this procedure in 1974
- **Nitroglycerin**—in 1846, Italian chemist Ascanio Soberero discovered this chemical explosive
- **The Zamboni machine**—the original ice-cleaning machine was invented by Italian America Frank Zamboni

JERSEY SHORE SOUNDBITE

There is definitely a numbers game when it comes to girls. As long as you keep calling, there will be success in your numbers game; it's just like anything. —THE SITUATION

31. You Can Collect the Most Phone Numbers During a Night Out, but You've Never Gotten a Date Out of It

To make the night a little more interesting, you and the boys play the old phone number game. Of course, you have your sacred little black book back at the house, hidden at the bottom of your sock draw, but those numbers are just guaranteed hookups that you know you can always turn to in a dire situation. Tonight is all about getting the digits, whether it is from a grenade or one of the hotties she is standing next to. Whoever gets the most numbers at the end of the night is a stud. You smooth talk some fine-looking ladies, and by the end of the night you've easily scored twenty to thirty numbers. However, when you try to use those numbers to get a date, you are sent to voicemail time and time again. It is either that or the chick picks up and doesn't have a clue who you are. Some words of advice for our favorite Guidos: Don't let your boys see you strike out—quit playing that stupid game.

> **PAISANO Says**
>
> **Psychiatrist:** I watch the news like everyone else. I know who you are, and I saw *Analyze This*. I don't need the ramifications that could arise from treating someone like yourself.
>
> **Tony Soprano:** *Analyze This*? Come on, it's a fucking comedy.

32. Your Ma Lights a Candle for You Every Time You Go Out

Your mother is the most devout Catholic you know. Her belief in God is even stronger than her belief in which Frank Sinatra song is the most romantic. You can always count on her to say an extra Hail Mary to save your soul. Knowing about your risqué behavior at certain nightclubs, your Mamma has things under control. Nothing better happen to her baby while having a night of fun out on the town, so Ma runs right down to the church and lights a candle. She will not only pray for you but for everyone you plan on seeing, sleeping with, or punching that night. All the saints will be called upon to protect you from STDs, unwanted pregnancy, alcohol poisoning, a broken nose, and a DUI. You better get your butt to mass in the morning to say thank you—no matter how hungover you are!

> **PAISANO Says**
>
> Sure, mom, I settle down with a nice girl every night, then I'm free the next morning. —**Tommy DeVito**, *Goodfellas*

TOUGH-GUY TRIVIA

Actors in *The Sopranos* have run afoul of the law. Michael Squicciarini, who played an enforcer in a couple episodes, was charged with a gangland hit before his death from natural causes. Robert Iler, who played A. J. Soprano, got into a couple of minor squabbles with the law. Lillo Brancato, who played Matt Bevalaqua, was sentenced to ten years in prison for robbery in January 2009.

33. You've Taken a Grenade for the Team

We've all seen her out there—the beast in the middle of the beauties. She is the butt of the jokes from all her "friends." She is either too sloppy or too sober. She is the grenade, and if she isn't getting any, neither is anyone else! Her group of hot friends at the bar will not leave her behind, so that means someone in your crew has to jump on the grenade and take one for the team, and tonight that is you, my friend. Your duties are honorable and well respected amongst the group. Generally if you were to be seen leaving the club with such a disaster, your blowout would be shaved off and you would be excommunicated from the group—but not tonight. Look at the bright side of this unfortunate situation, though: the grenade jumper is usually the only one that ends up actually getting laid.

JERSEY SHORE SOUNDBITE

When you go into battle, you need to have your friends with you so that just in case a grenade gets thrown at you, one of your buddies takes it first. —THE SITUATION

34. You've Gone to Church Still Drunk from the Night Before

You sure are regretting telling your parents that you would make it up from the Shore on Sunday morning for church. Now look at you, desperately chugging Gatorade with Jägermeister still on your breath. Last night at the club was crazy though...orange Guidettes were everywhere, you were rockin' your newest Ed Hardy gear, and the DJ was boomin'—but now you have to pay for it. You know, if you were not in your midthirties and still hitting the club, maybe we would feel bad for you. The amazing thing is, as rough as you look at the moment, with your clothes in shambles and the booze seeping through your pores, the blowout you spent a half an hour creating in the mirror last night before you hit the club is still in immaculate condition. I guess the folks will be proud of you for something. Miraculously, you make it through mass without blowing chunks and even managed to receive communion without falling over. However, you think Father O'Flanagan could sense what was really going on when he said, "The Body of Christ" and you opened your mouth and said "Jägerbomb."

> **WISE GUY WISECRACKS**
> *It was great to be Catholic and go to confession. You could start over every week.* —**Calogero, A Bronx Tale**

Guido Wisdom
La nostra famiglia è un cerchio di sostegno.
TRANSLATION: Our family is a circle of strength.

REAL OR FAKE?

Think you can spot a fake Guido? Bet you'll never guess which actor is really Italian and which isn't. Hint: Some are famous for playing Guidos, but we want to see if you can pick the real Italians from Hollywood's idea of what makes someone look and act Italian American.

1. Alan Alda

2. Bobby Darin

3. Cher

4. Jason Biggs

5. Rudolph Valentino

6. Peter Falk

7. Arthur Fonzarelli

8. Robert Blake

9. Henry Fonda

10. Nigella Lawson

QUIZ ANSWERS

1. **Yes.** Actor Alan Alda, immortalized as Hawkeye in TV's perennially funny *M.A.S.H.*, was born Alfonso D'Abruzzo, but his father, Alphonso Giovanni Giuseppe Roberto D'Abruzzo, had changed his name to Robert Alda to better assimilate into American culture.

2. **Yes.** Bobby Darin, a multitalented rock and roll idol of the 1950s and 60s, was born Walden Robert Cassotto. He grew up in the Bronx and didn't discover until he was grown that the grandmother who raised him was not his real mother—the woman he knew as his sister had given birth to him. Darin was hugely talented and was once married to America's sweetheart, Sandra Dee.

3. **No.** Although Cher won an Academy Award as best actress for her convincing and truly fabulous performance as an Italian woman breaking free from her scripted life in *Moonstruck*, Cher looks the part but is not Italian. Her father, John Sarkisian, was an Armenian refugee; her mother, Jackie Jean Crouch, was Cherokee, English, German, and Irish. Her husband and longtime manager, Sonny Bono, was Italian American.

4. **Yes.** Jason Biggs, who is best known for his comedic portrayal of Jim Levenstein in the American Pie films, is often cast in roles as a Jewish character. However, the Italian American Biggs grew up in Hasbrouck Heights, New Jersey.

5. **Yes.** Rudolph Valentino's birth name was Rodolfo Alfonso Rafaello Piero Filiberto Gugliemi di Valentina d'Antoguolla. He became Hollywood's first sex symbol and the first "Latin Lover," although he is best known for his portrayal of a sheik. Valentino died tragically at age thirty-one of a perforated ulcer. The poor darling fretted constantly about l'amore.

6. **No.** Despite his fabulous portrayal as the apparently bumbling yet brilliant detective Colombo on the long-running TV series of the same name, actor Peter Falk is not Italian. Falk is Russian and Polish, with a mix of Hungarian and Czech further back in his ancestry.

7. **Yes/No.** The character Arthur Fonzarelli was Italian, but Henry Winkler, the actor who portrayed "The Fonz" on Happy Days, is not Italian. Winkler's parents immigrated to America from Germany in 1939.

8. **Yes.** Robert Blake was born Michael James Vincenzo Gubitosi. Best known for his role in *Baretta*, Blake began his career as Mickey in the Our Gang shorts shown widely on TV in the 1950s and 60s.

9. **Yes.** Henry Fonda's family originated in Genoa, Italy, migrating to the Netherlands and then to America in the 1600s, settling in a town that is now known as Fonda, New York. In 1999, the American Film Institute named the Academy Award–winning Fonda the sixth-greatest male star of all time.

10. **No.** Famous chef Nigella Lawson may look Italian, and may even have an Italian-sounding name, but she is of Jewish descent and was raised in England. Her recipes might be misleading since this vixen can cook up a storm.

35. You've Hosted Sunday Dinner but Made Your Mom Bring the Food

In your family, hosting Sunday night dinner is a rite of passage. It means you are finally grown up because normally you cannot host until you have a family of your own. So once again it's Sunday afternoon and you've invited your whole family over for a meal. However, you must put in an emergency call to Ma on Saturday night asking if she could bring all of the food. You'll take care of the wine. You know she will not see lugging half her kitchen and most of the contents of her refrigerator to your house as a burden; anything for her little baby. Even though dinner is at two, she shows up at seven in the morning to prepare the feast. Sunday dinner is not just a roast chicken, see. It's like any other family's Thanksgiving spread. The great thing about your Ma is she still cuts up your meat for you. And you know that while everyone is enjoying the delicious meal, she will be in the kitchen doing the dishes. Well that was easy—you might as well host every Sunday dinner for the rest of your life!

Guido Wisdom
La vita è come un albero di natale, c'è sempre qualcuno che rompe le palle.
TRANSLATION: Life is like a Christmas tree, there's always someone who breaks the balls.

36. You Have a Collection of Pictures of Yourself Flexing in the Mirror

They are all over your phone. They are all over your room. They are all over your MySpace and Facebook. You have so many pictures of yourself flexing in different positions that it is embarassing—to say the least. You think that girls are just going to drool over your flexed biceps, featuring a new rosary bead tattoo wrapping around it, but really they are just laughing, along with everyone else that is looking at these cheeseball pics. You like to turn the camera at an angle, or hold your puppy, or do the "no T-shirt but still wearing a baseball cap" look, but no matter how you snap that picture in the mirror using your poor-quality cell phone camera, you look like a big idiot. If there is anything more ridiculous than the pictures of a shirtless you all over your MySpace page, it's all those pictures of your rice burner and the late '90s Mustang that you got painted at Maaco and the "bumpin'" sound system you got at Walmart. Just keep it to one headshot and maybe a picture of your family. That is all we need to understand who you are—because really there is nothing too deep behind those "stunner" shades.

TOUGH-GUY TRIVIA

The famous dinner scene with Tommy's mother in *Goodfellas* was almost completely improvised, including Tommy asking his mother if he could borrow her butcher's knife and Jimmy's "hoof" comment.

37. A Wife Beater Is a Permanent Part of Your Wardrobe

No Guido, no matter his weight class, is complete without his signature white tank top. A staple of any outfit, whether by itself or under the club shirt that has five buttons too many undone, the chest you have spent countless hours at the gym building looks great when it's barely being covered. You don't have to worry, either; that spot of marinara just adds character. So versatile when it comes to your lifestyle, this simple piece of clothing can help when you are trying to show off your sick ink or for creating those perfect pictures for Facebook. The gold chain with obnoxious gold cross hangs just right between your glistening pecs, and lifting it up to show off your six-pack is a lot easier than one of those long button-up polos. Thank god for the man who created this essential part of the Guido wardrobe. He must have been Italian.

GUIDO HOT SPOTS

Martin Scorsese's first movie, *Mean Streets*, was partly based on his years growing up in Manhattan's Little Italy. But by the time it came to shoot the movie, Scorsese had to film in Brooklyn to get a real Italian neighborhood feel, as Little Italy had become a tourist destination and had lost the authentic neighborhood feel.

THINGS YOU WOULD KNOW IF YOU WERE REALLY A GUIDO

Guidos have their own set of rules, and anyone who grows up in a Guido family knows the ropes—the spoken and unspoken truths

about what it really means to be Italian American. A few of the tenets are as follows:

- If you're not 100 percent Italian, you're not really Italian.
- Every Italian family is full of secrets, most of which are rarely kept.
- Cursing on holidays is verboten.
- Respect is everything. Kissing someone's ring is respectful. Popping someone in the face is not.

TOUGH-GUY TRIVIA

Fat Clemenza makes a mean gravy. In the original script, Coppolla wrote, "Clemenza browns some sausage." While reading the script, Mario Puzo crossed out "browns" and replaced it with "fries," writing in the margin, "Gangsters don't brown."

38. Your Goal in Life Is to Become a DJ or a Bartender

When it comes to occupations, you always shoot for the stars. You started as a delivery driver at your local house of pizza, then you moved up in the world to a construction job that really "busts your ass" during the week. So when it comes time to hit the club on the weekend, you go all out and always find yourself staring at the bartender and DJ, trying to picture what it would be like to hold such an exciting position in the "scene." You spend countless hours in the basement pretending to be a DJ with the music-mixing computer program you bought off of eBay. Then when there is a house party, you act as the self-appointed bartender and mix up drinks for everyone, even if you are awful at it (which you are). Sometimes you even mix up a batch of that signature creation of yours, which is really just light rum with every kind of fruit juice you have on hand. Maybe someday a club owner will realize your talents and you will be the first ever bartending disk jockey . . . but don't hold your breath, Guido.

JERSEY SHORE SOUNDBITE

I'm a bartender. I do great things.—ANGELINA

Girls love a DJ, so once they see me behind the wheels of steel over there, doing my thing . . . watch out. —PAULY D

39. You Know the Names of All the Dancers at the Local Strip Club

You and the crew are out at the bar and the place is just filled with gre-
nades and alpha males, so you decide it is time to make an executive
decision: everyone into the Beemer and it's off to the strip club. You walk
in and all the girls know your name—and how loose you are with your wallet after just two shots of Jäger.

You think you are the man with
all these girls on you, but you
are just an idiot. You remember
seeing in some rap video once
that "making it rain" seems to
be all the craze at the moment,
so, sure enough, you go up to
the second level of the club
and begin throwing dollar bills
down all over the stage—which
you think instantly makes you a
celebrity. Instead, security has determined that you and the rest of your
earring-clad crew are too intoxicated and drag you out by the straps of
your tank top. But you're not concerned because all the dancers "have
your number memorized," so they can call you when they get off their
shift later on. Isn't that right?

"PAISANO Says

My daughter got off on this femi-
nist rant. She told me it's demean-
ing for a girl to be working at the
Bing. The fact that these girls make
$1,500 a week has no bearing with
my principessa. —**Silvio Dante,**
The Sopranos **"**

40. You've Made a Special Playlist on Your iPod Full of Your Favorite House Music

The sweet jams do not have to end when the club closes. You've downloaded all of your favorite thumping beats from iTunes and have the ultimate house mix on your iPod. From techno to triphop, if it has a beat that will make your ears throb and is loud enough to feel in your gut, it is sure as hell going on that mix. And you cannot just have the version they play in the club. You need the "never released, Japanese import only" version. You even have the same song ten times but with a different DJ's house mix for each. Now you can practice your dance skills in the shower, at the gym, and in the car. We all know what a great time you are having because we can feel the bass from your system all the way down the street. Forget the fact that you can see the little old lady next to you turn down her hearing aid or the baby in the car behind you start to cry because the bass is scaring him. Just keep blasting those beats for the whole neighborhood to hear, 'cause this party is just gettin' started.

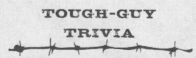

TOUGH-GUY
TRIVIA

Tony Sirico, aka Paulie "Walnuts" Gaultieri, only agreed to sign on for *The Sopranos* if David Chase guaranteed that his character would not end up being a "rat."

YOU THINK YOU KNOW *A BRONX TALE*?

You may not have grown up on the streets of the Bronx during the 1960s, but you have seen *A Bronx Tale* so many times you feel like you belonged in one of those doo-wop groups on the street corner, experiencing everyday life on the streets. Take the quiz below to see if you know the difference between the guy that used only three fingers and the guy whose shadow once killed a dog.

1. What is the name of the of the Beatles' song playing when the biker gang comes into town?

A. "Yellow Submarine"

B. "Hey Jude"

C. "Come Together"

D. "Eleanor Rigby"

2. Who both starred in and directed *A Bronx Tale*?

A. Chazz Palminteri

B. Frank Capra

C. Lillo Brancato Jr.

D. Robert De Niro

3. What is Calogero's last name?

A. Anello

B. Giordano

C. Lorenzo

D. Mush

4. What section of the Bronx does Calogero and his family live in?
A. East Tremont
B. Fordham
C. Hunts Point
D. City Island

5. What is the name of the social club that "C" and his friends from school have?
A. The Spot
B. The Three Kings
C. Deuces Wild
D. Four Aces

6. Who was Sonny's main man?
A. Frankie Coffeecake
B. Jimmy Whispers
C. Tony Toupee
D. Jojo the Whale

7. What did Phil the Peddler like to call everybody?
A. Joe
B. Captain
C. Governor
D. Mary

8. What was Lorenzo's occupation?
A. Bus driver
B. Butcher
C. Taxicab driver
D. Firefighter

9. Whose writings did Sonny read while in prison?

A. Giannozzo Manetti

B. Coluccio Salutati

C. Niccolò Machiavelli

D. Leonardo Bruni

10. Where was Calogero's favorite bus stop?

A. Webster Avenue

B. City Island

C. The horse track

D. Fordham

11. How many times did Sonny shoot the man in the beginning?

A. 1

B. 2

C. 3

D. 4

12. Who is the greatest baseball player to ever live, according to Lorenzo?

A. Joe Dimaggio

B. Babe Ruth

C. Mickey Mantle

D. Lou Gehrig

13. How many great women are you "allowed" in your lifetime, according to Sonny?

A. 2

B. 3

C. 4

D. 6

14. What do the black men throw at the social club in retaliation for the beatings?

A. Rocks

B. Glass bottles

C. Eggs

D. Paint

15. What is the name of the club that Sonny and his men reside at?

A. Chez Bippy

B. The Deli

C. Fordham Social

D. The Lounge

16. How many passes in a row does Calogero throw when he plays dice at the club?

A. 7

B. 9

C. 11

D. 13

17. What is the name of the horse that everyone bets on at the track, including Eddie Mush?

A. Decidedly

B. Kryptonite

C. Proud Clarion

D. Majestic Prince

18. What was the reason Jimmy Whispers gave to the biker gang as to why they had to leave?

A. They were being loud.

B. They were not dressed properly.

C. Their money was not green.

D. Bikers were not allowed at the Chez Bippy.

19. What was Jane's brother's name?
   A. Tommy
   B. Mikey
   C. Jamal
   D. Willie

20. How much money did Calogero's mother find in his dresser?
   A. $200
   B. $300
   C. $600
   D. $1000

QUIZ ANSWERS

2: D; 3: A; 4: B; 5: C; 6: B; 7: D; 8: A; 9: C; 10: B; 11: D; 12: A; 13: B; 14: C; 15: A; 16: C; 17: B; 18: B; 19: D; 20: C

41. You've Gone "Fishing" for Girls

It's Friday night and you are hanging off the balcony of your Shore house with your buddies trying to hook a honey. You throw out a line and hope something bites. Catcalling goes back quite a ways, but you and your friends have taken it to an even more humiliating level. You just stand in a line on the balcony and yell at chicks. You try to pull off that Guido charm, but it is hard to do from twelve feet up in the air. What girl would not want to be whistled and yelled at by a bunch of goombahs ogling them like pieces of hot prosciutto? You are sure to find a quality girl that way. However, if a Guidette is dim enough to find that flattering, maybe you deserve each other. You end up yelling back and forth "No, you come up here," "NO, you come down here," until someone gives up and just walks away or agrees to

“ PAISANO Says

Christopher Moltisanti: I'm going to hell,

Tony Soprano: You're not going anywhere but home.

Christopher Moltisanti: I crossed over to the other side.

Tony Soprano: You what?

Christopher Moltisanti: I saw the tunnel and the white light . . . and I saw my father in hell. The Emerald Piper, that's our hell. It's an Irish bar where it's St. Patrick's Day every day forever. **”**

go up or down to meet the other. Just remember, some girls look much prettier from far away, so you're taking a chance when you go fishing. You never know when you have a grenade on your hands. So swing back and throw that line—maybe you will hook a prize winner you can mount.

42. You Buy Condoms in Bulk

It is time to pack for your summer down at the Shore, and one of the most essential items on the list is a fifty-count box of condoms. With drunk Guidettes running around in their low-cut "Italian Princess" shirts and super-tight Juicy Couture jeans, you know the temptation to land one of these dime pieces will be overwhelming, but hopefully just as overwhelming is your desire to avoid one of the many STDs these female counterparts to the Guido often carry. You figure by keeping two in your wallet, two in the glove box of the BMW, and the other forty-six you have yet to use in your sock draw at the Shore house, you will be prepared if the occasion arises. By the end of the summer, you've secretly thrown half of them away so your roommates do not think that you have been failing all over the place, but at least they are going into the trash and not being used to jump on a grenade!

Guidos Versus Goombahs

Guidos and goombahs are two completely different things. How do you know which one you are? Check out the descriptions below and guess for yourself.

Guidos

Guidos are what many today might call metrosexuals. They typically had mothers who fussed over their appearance so much that they grew up to be fussy, too. They are typically obsessed about their appearance and spend enormous amounts of time blow-drying their hair, dressing to the nines, and showing off. Remember the scene in

Saturday Night Fever when John Travolta, as Tony Manero, spent forever primping before the mirror, making sure every strand of his hair was perfectly coiffed? And then, when he went downstairs for dinner and his father got mad and clapped him in the head, and Tony wailed "Would ya watch the hair? Ya know, I spend a long time on my hair, and he hits it." That delicious Travolta characterization portended the modern-day Guido.

Today's Guidos are younger, drive Hummers or BMWs, and have broken free of the tradition of wearing a horn dangling on a showy gold necklace with their shirts open halfway down their chests to show it off against exposed skin. Modern-day Guidos are still vain, but they show it off by frequenting tanning salons and wearing thick, 18-karat gold crosses on a chain. The sons of convicted Mafia chief John Gotti, as they were portrayed in episodes of the reality TV show *Growing Up Gotti*, personified the modern Guido image.

Goombahs

Goombahs are not as sophisticated, not as metrosexual. They are usually schlumpy guys with big bellies who laze around drinking beer and shoveling pasta into their mouths. As children—and often well into their adulthood, or until the poor woman drops—their mothers overfed them and pampered them by making their favorite foods and pushing them to "mangia, mangia." Small surprise then that they are focused on feeding their souls through food. They are usually blue-collar workers or those guys who took over their father's construction business. They tend to stick close to home and hearth, often living in the same house or right around the corner from their mammas.

43. You've Created a Signature Drink

"Didn't you know? Back home I'm known as Tony the Bartender!" Every drunken Guido loves to pretend that he is a bartender, because he is pretty much convinced that that little piece of paper he got from the Tri-State Bartending Academy makes him an official connoisseur of the cocktail. No, it absolutely does not, but he likes to pretend he knows what he's doing! Not only is he in the middle of the party with bottles of Jägermeister, Bacardi, and twenty fruit juices surrounding him, but he has already broken four margarita glasses trying to be Tom Cruise in *Cocktail*. Now that everyone is pretty much fed up with this idiot's alcoholic antics, he decides it's time to pull out his signature special—Tony's Tongue Twister. Created a few summers ago when all he had for alcohol was what he could find in his parents' cabinet, whatever juice was in the fridge, and the six-pack of Redbull on his nightstand, Tony came up with what he thinks is the key to having a killer night. Lucky for him, he was able to throw together a batch before he came out tonight, and now everyone is getting "twisted" on this disastrous concoction. Too bad he didn't bring along the club mix CD he just made—then he would really be king of the party.

GUIDO HOT SPOTS

The hospital scenes in *The Godfather* were filmed in two different locations: the exterior scenes were filmed at the Bellevue Hospital, and the interior shots were filmed at the New York Eye and Ear Infirmary in Manhattan, New York City.

44. You've Asked for a Track Suit for Your Birthday

Your birthday is just around the corner, and at the top of your wish list is the king of all outfits in the Guido world. Sometimes referred to as the Staten Island tuxedo, this gem of the clothing world is as common to the Guido and Guidette as a white tank top. Young and old, big and small, these two-piece wonders, often made of velour, can be worn to bed, casually around town, or even out to the clubs. How versatile! The mobster wouldn't be complete standing outside the butcher shop in his white running shoes and big gold chains without a baby blue track suit. Adri-ana can't think of an easier outfit to slip in and out of at the tanning salon than her bright pink Juicy Couture track suit with "Baby" written across the ass. So every year, when it comes that special day when this world was blessed with baby Vinny or baby Alessandra, you know they'll be asking for at least one new track suit, because what "real" Italian is complete without one?

WISE GUY WISECRACKS
Q. *What did the barber say to the Italian kid?*
A. *Do you want your hair cut or should I just change the oil?*

GUESS THAT GANGSTER #4

He was the mob boss whose assassination in 1985 prompted the ascendancy of John Gotti to power and prominence. The hit was an easy one, something a shrewd Mafia don should have seen coming. Although he was not above using the traditional Mafia business practices of murder and mayhem, he brought the Gambino crime family into more legitimate businesses. But he did not have the survival instincts to save his life. John Gotti was the man who arranged the hit, and he became the head of the Gambino family afterward. (See back of the book for the answer.)

THE ULTIMATE GUIDETTE ESSENTIALS CHECKLIST

No respectable Guidette will walk out of the house without these essential items. If you're a true Guidette, you'll follow these guidelines.

- ☐ Acrylic nails
- ☐ French manicure or fake jewels glued on the toenails
- ☐ Hair extensions
- ☐ Highlights
- ☐ Bronzer
- ☐ Fake eyelashes
- ☐ Red lipstick
- ☐ Lip gloss
- ☐ At least one piece of clothing with an animal print
- ☐ Fake Louis Vuitton or Fendi purse
- ☐ Chewing gum
- ☐ A very small dog in its own carrying case
- ☐ Super high-heeled shoes
- ☐ Tanning lotion or baby oil
- ☐ An Italian horn on a gold chain
- ☐ A gold ring that says Italian Princess

45. Your Week Doesn't Begin until You Restock Your Cold Cuts

Guidos and cold cuts—it's a love affair that cannot be explained. Open any Guido's refrigerator bin and there will be a week's worth of hot or sweet capicola (Guidos say gabbagool), proscuitto, mortadella, salami, and a variety of other smoked meats; all the fixings for a mean Italian grinder. They are the perfect choice after a hard workout at the gym or a midnight snack after a night of drinking at the club. At any given time during the day, if you show up at the deli you are bound to run into five of your cousins, two childhood friends, and three neighbors. It is the cool place to be on a Sunday afternoon. The butcher knows your name, your parents' names, and even how you did on your last history test in school. He always wraps you up something nice on the side and tells you to take it home to the folks, on the house, of course. You still get that sample slice of mortadella too, that same slice you've had handed to you over the counter since you were just a miniature Guido. The meat deli is just your home away from home.

GUIDO HOT SPOTS

The mob bosses in *Casino*'s courthouse scenes are never named, nor is it made clear what cities they represent. In real life, the bosses who were indicted for skimming the casinos in Vegas included Nick Civella, boss of Kansas City; Joe Aiuppa and Jackie Cerone, boss and underboss of the Chicago Outfit; and Frank Balistrieri, boss of Milwaukee.

46. You Still Tease or Scrunch Your Hair

Just in case no one told you, it's not 1989 anymore. Teasing is out, but that does not stop you from having the highest hair out there, especially if you hail from Jersey. It hits the roof of your car while you are driving, you have hit people in the face with your wild mane, and you still buy bottles of AquaNet. You have probably contributed to the hole in the ozone layer, but you don't even know what that means, so it's okay. You have the hair routine down to a science. It should be—you have had twenty years to perfect it. If you are not a teaser, you are a scruncher. Jump out of the shower, run a comb through your locks, load up on mousse and gel, then tip your head over and scrunch away for a good twenty minutes. Every five minutes or so, flip the hair to see how it is coming along and then continue to scrunch. A little beachy wave is one thing, but your head is shellacked. It's not going anywhere. When you touch it, it crunches. Now you know you have perfection. Thanks to *Jersey Shore*'s Snooki, you have a new hairstyle to rock—the Poof. It takes some skill to create such a bump, but if you do, you will be queen of the club. Remember, the bigger the better!

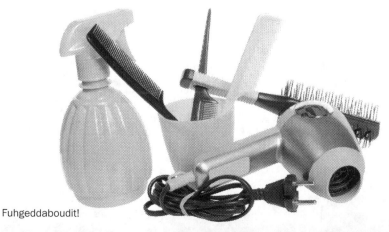

NAME THAT GUIDO SPORTS STAR

You think the only good sports stars are Guidos. Let's see if you can match the Guido to his famous nickname.

1. Yankee Clipper

2. The Scooter

3. Comeback Kid

4. Yogi

5. Mr. Baseball

6. Espo

7. Brockton Blockbuster

8. JoePa

9. Tony O

QUIZ ANSWERS

1. **Joseph Paul DiMaggio** (Giuseppe Paolo DiMaggio Jr.), the "Greatest Living Player" of baseball, was the son of Sicilian immigrants who settled in California. DiMaggio played baseball for the New York Yankees for thirteen years, where he sustained a fifty-six-game hitting streak in 1941, the longest in baseball history, and was voted the American League's Most Valuable Player three times (1939, 1941, and 1947). He was also known as Joltin Joe and was immortalized in Billy Joel's hit song "We Didn't Start the Fire" and Paul Simon's "Mrs. Robinson."

2. **Phil Rizzuto,** the record-setting shortstop for the New York Yankees from 1941 until 1954 (minus two years serving in the Navy during WW II), was known for his agility as a shortstop. He was considered a key member of ten Yankee pennant-winning teams and nine World Series classics and was the American League's most valuable player. When he retired, Rizzuto went on to become a sports announcer and eventually "the voice of the Yankees."

3. **Quarterback Joe Montana** (Montana is an Americanized form of the surname Montani, which comes from northern Italy) completed the greatest Super Bowl drive of all time, eight complete passes in two minutes and thirty seconds, in 1984. While quarterback for the San Francisco 49ers, Montana's team won four Super Bowl titles, and he was named Most Valuable Player in three of those four Super Bowl games.

4. **Yogi Berra**, the son of Pietro and Paulina Berra, immigrants from Italy, played for teams that won a total of fourteen pennants and ten World Series, a record no other player has matched. One of baseball's greatest catchers, he was voted the American League's Most Valuable Player three times (1951, 1954, and 1959). After

seventeen years with the New York Yankees, Berra went on to manage both the New York Yankees and the New York Mets. In 1964, when the New York Yankees won the American pennant, Berra became the first Italian American baseball manager to win a league championship.

5. **Tommy Lasorda** spent fifty years with the Dodgers, the second-longest tenure with one team. He served in the roles of player, scout, coach, manager, and vice president. He led the Dodgers to five division titles, three National League titles, and the 1981 World Championship. Lasorda was named Manager of the Year four times and managed in three World Series and three All-Star games.

6. **Phil Esposito** played hockey for the Chicago Blackhawks, Boston Bruins, and New York Rangers for eighteen years. He once scored seventy-six goals in a single season and was inducted into the Hockey Hall of Fame.

7. **Rocky Marciano** (Rocco Francis Marchegiano), the son of Pierino and Pasqualina Marchegiano, was the only undefeated heavyweight boxing champion in history. Marciano won the heavyweight crown in Philadelphia in 1952 and defended his title six times before retiring in 1956, with a 49-0 record that included forty-three knockouts. He was elected to the Boxing Hall of Fame in 1959 and died in a plane crash ten years later. He hailed from Brockton, Massachusetts, hence the nickname.

8. **Joe Paterno** is the head coach of the Penn State football team and has led his team to twenty-two major bowl games and four perfect seasons. He is credited with producing many All-American players and forty-eight players who joined the NFL. Chosen Coach of the Year three times, this coach won more than 80 percent of his games.

9. **Tony Esposito**, Phil Esposito's younger brother, was one of the greatest goaltenders of all time. He played for the Chicago Blackhawks for fifteen years where he was nicknamed Tony O for his famous shutouts. Voted National League All-Star a record ten times, Esposito later became general manager of the New York Rangers.

47. You Wax Every Stray Hair on Your Body

It is the curse of the Italians—you are hairier than a chimp. You were just a preteen Guidette when you started having to battle that mustache. But it's okay. You've got a routine you follow religiously. It began with bottles of Nair in your bathroom at the tender age of twelve—or if you were really unlucky, ten or eleven. You pour that shit on and wait for the burn. When you smell like cooked meat, you wash it off. The problem is solved—until next week. Now that you are older and wiser, you can pay people to remove your hair. We're not talking about a little brow or lip wax. You get the whole package. When it comes to the nether regions, you only trust Helga the wonder waxer. She can get in and out of there in less than three minutes. You'll feel like a hairless rat, but that's what you were going for right? You even wax the nontraditional body parts like your forearms and your toes. Guidos and Guidettes alike know the importance of being able to slide off each other like a kids at the water park. It may be the curse of the Italians, but you make it work and would not change who you are for all the gabbagool in the world.

GUIDO HOT SPOTS

The most famous scene in *Goodfellas* may be the walk into the Copa through the kitchen. The Steadicam follows Henry and his soon-to-be-wife Karen from the streets of Manhattan through the kitchen of the hottest nightclub in town. This widely praised shot is coupled with another Steadicam scene, this one introducing all of the mobsters around Henry Hill as he enters the Bamboo Lounge.

WHY GUIDOS LOVE THEIR MAMMAS

There are mothers—and then there are Italian mothers. Everyone knows the grand passion every Italian mother possesses—for her progeny. Italian mothers are different from other mothers, mostly in the drama department. You know you're dealing with an Italian mother if . . .

- She calls you at 11 p.m. just to make sure you got enough to eat at dinner—and you're thirty-five.
- She continually reminds you that your biological clock is ticking and it's time to "get on the ball"—and you're still in college.
- She comes to visit you on "vacation"—and spends the entire time happily dusting your furniture, organizing your closets, and scrubbing your floors.
- She finds out you haven't had a date in six months—and says a rosary a day until you agree to go out on a blind date with her hairdresser's cousin's old college roommate.
- She pushes macaroni and gravy on you at every opportunity, claiming that "you're too thin since you left home"—when in fact you've gained thirty pounds.

48. You Proudly Display Your Thong When You Go to the Club

As if it were some strange form of juicehead bait, you let that thong show all night long. Hell, you might as well not wear any pants because you are not leaving much to the imagination when everyone can see the thong strings riding up on your hips, not to mention when you decide to drop it like it's hot and bring back the butterfly as you undulate your way to the ground. We know you mean business when you break out the faux-diamond-studded or pleather thong. And when the drinks start flowing, you cannot help showing all of us what you and your under-

WISE GUY WISECRACKS
Q. *What's an innuendo?*
A. *An Italian suppository*

wear are made of when you do backflips on the floor while wearing a miniskirt. Now that is pure class. Guidos, watch out; she is not playing around tonight. Someday you are going to look back and wonder how many pairs of your prized thongs were hanging on juicehead "walls of accomplishment" all over the Shore.

JERSEY SHORE SOUNDBITE

This little shrimp thing is like bopping all around on the circle and like doing her thing, doing backwards flips with her thong hanging out; her whole crotch is in the air. —SAMMI

49. You Submit Pictures of You and Your Crew to Area Night Clubs for Use on Their Websites

So it was another bumpin' night at the mainstream club you only heard about from some magazine, and you and the crew were there fist-pumping to the beat and throwing back Heinekens like it was your job. Lucky for you, and the dance club scene, there was a photographer snapping pictures of all the Guido and Guidette nonsense that takes place in every club on the Shore. So the next morning it is right to the Internet to check out the nightlife websites and see if you and the boys were captured tearing it up. You find a few good ones of everyone with their arms around each other, drinks in hand, with peace signs being thrown up by half of you and puckered lips and ab shots being offered by the rest. You immediately e-mail all the clubs you frequent and submit all the "great" shots of you and the crew being absolute douchebags—because you symbolize all that these clubs stand for and they would be "lucky" to have such representatives featured on their homepage. Hope that works out for you . . . it would be a great thing to be able to tell all the girls in the club that you and all your similarly dressed friends are on the website of the club they are standing in.

JERSEY SHORE SOUNDBITE

When I go into the club I have a game plan. I don't wanna waste my time and take home a girl that just wants to hang out, I just wanna get to the business . . . so you light it up and then you move on and at the end of the night you see who you end up with. —PAULY D

YOU THINK YOU KNOW *JERSEY SHORE?*

This fun-loving bunch made you fist-pump your way to the club so you could act just like them. No one knows how to party harder than the cast from *Jersey Shore*. Think you know all there is to know about the show? Take the quiz below and test your skills.

1. After a night of dancing and cheating on her boyfriend with Pauly, J-WOWW heads back to the house before anyone else and grabs a snack. What does she eat?
A. Ham
B. Sausages
C. Pizza
D. Ziti

2. Vinny gets a bacterial infection after dancing in the club the first night they move in. What does he get?
A. Impetigo
B. Pinkeye
C. Athlete's foot
D. Urinary tract infection

3. What does Pauly call Danielle, the stalker from the boardwalk?
A. Crazy face
B. Psycho bitch
C. Stage-five clinger
D. The obsession

4. Which girl got punched in the face by a guy at the bar?

A. Angelina

B. Sammi

C. J-WOWW

D. Snooki

5. Ron concocts a special drink before they go out. What does he call the drink?

A. The Master Blaster

B. Ronalicious

C. The Punch

D. Ron-Ron Juice

6. On the way home from the club, Ronnie and Sammi get in a fight and he makes fun of a part of her body. She is devastated that he would make fun of her about it. Which part of her body was it?

A. Her big toe

B. Her small breasts

C. Her big butt

D. Her frizzy hair

7. Pauly has a piercing that he's only shown to J-WOWW. What does he have pierced?

A. His nipple

B. His butt cheek

C. His penis

D. The inside of his thigh

8. The group goes on a vacation at the end of the season. Where do they go for the weekend?

A. Cabo

B. Vegas

C. Miami

D. Atlantic City

9. What is Ronnie's number one rule while he's down at the Jersey Shore?

A. "Drink until you black out."

B. "Get in a fight at least once a night."

C. "Never fall in love at the Jersey Shore."

D. "Work hard; play harder."

10. Which dark-haired hottie does Angelina compare herself to?

A. Kim Kardashian

B. Alyssa Milano

C. Angelina Jolie

D. Paula Abdul

11. Mike's trying to hook up with some girl he picked up when her friend says that she has to go home. He calls her an interesting nickname. What does he call her?

A. Lady Hater

B. Freckles McGee

C. Worrywort

D. Mood Killer

12. The roomies had a very strange phone in the shape of an animal. What kind of animal is it?

A. A pig

B. A cow

C. A moose

D. A duck

13. What state is Pauly D from?

   A. Maryland

   B. California

   C. Rhode Island

   D. Florida

14. Snooki gets grossed out when the boys try and cook which sea creature?

   A. A lobster

   B. A clam

   C. A crab

   D. A squid

15. What kind of store do the roommates have to work in while they stay at the Shore house?

   A. A liquor store

   B. A T-shirt store

   C. A video store

   D. A convenience store

16. Mike makes a concoction to put under Vinnie's bed as revenge. What does he call it?

   A. Playerade

   B. Grosserade

   C. Smellerade

   D. Haterade

17. Mike also plays a joke on Snooki and hides something under her bed. What does he hide?

   A. Pickles

   B. Condoms

C. Smelly socks

D. A pair of his underwear

18. Why does Vinnie think he is going to get kicked out the house?

A. He beat up one of his roommates

B. He made out with his landlord's girlfriend

C. He was late for work

D. He trashed his room

19. Whose mom came over and brought dinner for the entire house?

A. Ron

B. Sammi

C. Snooki

D. Vinny

20. Pauly's stalker bought him a shirt with a saying on it. What did it say?

A. I "heart" Jewish girls

B. I'm with stupid

C. I'm in love with you

D. Will you marry me?

QUIZ ANSWERS

1: A; 2: B; 3: C; 4: D; 5: D; 6: A; 7: C; 8: D; 9: B; 10: A; 11: B; 12: D; 13: C; 14: A; 15: B; 16: D; 17: A; 18: B; 19: A; 20: A

50. You Regularly Get Kicked Out of Night Clubs but Just Move to the Next

When it comes to dance clubs on the Shore, you have your pick of the Guido-filled litter. You know that if the scene in any one of these house-music-bumping, strobe-light-flashing grind-fests is not suited to your particular tastes, you can just jump on over to the next dance club filled with the same exact people and the same exact music. After throwing back a few and getting your beer muscles all juiced up, you decide to leave this club in style—by being tossed out by security. As starting a fight with another alpha male in your vicinity is just customary Guido behavior, you pick a fight with the closest guy wearing a Tapout shirt, claiming that he must think he's a tough guy if he's wearing the shirt and he should prove it in the middle of the dance floor. Before the first fist is thrown, security has come over and broken up what would have been quite the slapfest—and you are being dragged out the front door. After a quick check of the hair and making sure you

didn't lose the faux Dolce & Gabbana earrings you just bought, you simply get into the line at the next club.

GUIDO HOT SPOTS

The Sopranos **was filmed on location throughout New Jersey, but the interior scenes were filmed at a sound stage in Queens, New York, located at Silvercup Studios. Some cities refused to allow the show to be filmed there, but others, like Kearney, Caldwell, and Lodi, embraced the notoriety and gave the show the authenticity it needed.**

51. You've Created Your Own Nickname and Tried to Copyright It

Paulie Walnuts. The Situation. Big Pussy. Snooki. Johnny Roastbeef. Frankie Coffeecake. All the great Guidos have a great nickname. Chances are if you have any sort of noticeably strange physical characteristic, it will work itself into a nickname (Babyface, Little Feet, Big Nose). Another way to know if you have a great moniker is if it can be shortened into one syllable (Snooki becomes Snooks, Sniks; Big Pussy becomes Puss). Guidos love to come up with shorter versions of nicknames. Soon The Situation will become The S.I.T.—you get the picture. You've even decided that your nickname is so important no one else should be able to use it for profit. So you fill out the paperwork and get that sucker trademarked. There is no way you will have the same name as anyone else on God's green earth. Just hope your precious moniker is not already trademarked. When Mike "The Situation" Sorrentino tried to copyright "The Situation," he found out someone already filed for a trademark—his brother who owns a porn company! That is a rough situation.

SNOOKI©

PAULIE WALNUTS©

FRANKIE COFFEECAKE©

⟨⟨ PAISANO Says

They called him Frankie Coffeecake because his face looked like a Drake's coffee cake. He was tough to look at. His name was Jimmy Whispers and he was Sonny's main man. They called him Whispers because everything was a secret to him. Eddie Mush was a degenerate gambler. He was also the biggest loser in the whole world. They called him Mush because everything he touched turned to mush. He would go to the racetrack and the teller would give him his tickets already ripped up. JoJo the Whale, as they say, you didn't walk with JoJo, you walked among him. If you stared at JoJo long enough, you'd see him get fatter by the hour. Legend has it his shadow once killed a dog. They called him Tony Toupee because he wore the worst hairpiece in the world. —**Calogero, *A Bronx Tale*** ⟩⟩

BIG PUSSY©

THE SITUATION©

JOHNNY ROASTBEEF©

52. You Say Sangweech Instead of Sandwich

"Hey Gino, make me an eggplant sangweech, and if you leave off the hot peppers, I'll break your legs." Somewhere down the line of famous Italian phrases, sandwich turned to sangweech. You grew up saying sangweech, and your non-Italian friends all made fun of you. They even try and get you to say it for no reason just for a laugh. Stick with your own kind and you can avoid the humiliation. When you drive by the local deli, they specifically advertise "toasted Italian sangweeches." How are you supposed to know that sangweech isn't an actual word? Your pop has been saying it since you were in diapers. If you're from the East Coast, you might have said grinder as well. Whatever you call it, there's nothing like a mean sangweech to get you through the day.

> **PAISANO Says**
>
> **Mary DeAngelis:** (bell rings) Oh my God!!! Who could that be!!!
>
> **Carmela Soprano:** It's the Boston Strangler . . . Jesus, Ma.

GUIDO HOT SPOTS

In *The Godfather* the shots of Corleone, Sicily, were actually Savoca, Sicily. Corelone was too developed in the early 1970s.

GUESS THAT GANGSTER #5

This mob boss died in a very public manner. He had the audacity to found the Italian-American Civil Rights League. This organization, founded by a Mafioso, was meant to combat the negative stereotypes that Italian Americans all have some connection to the Mafia. The other, more shrewd, Mafia dons did not like the light of publicity on them in any way, as this would do more damage than good. He was shot at his own rally in New York's Columbus Circle. He did not die outright but tragically lingered, living as essentially a vegetable for seven years. (See back of the book for the answer.)

53. You and Ten of Your Friends Have Crammed into a Shore House for the Summer

Oh, summers on the Shore—it has become nearly a ritual for every Guido and Guidette. Your summers have been defined by the drinking, partying, fighting, and dancing that is now commonplace on the Jersey Shore. Since the first summer you were of legal age, you've done things in your rented Shore house that would make your ancestors from the Other Side roll over in their graves. The living conditions are less than stellar, mostly due to the fact that you have ten inebriated goombahs living under one roof that are far more concerned with their hair than the trash being taken out regularly. It's like being in college all over again—not that any of you ever went in the first place. Though a lot of you may be searching for love on the Shore on these crazy and wild summers, none of you ever finds it, and you usually end up settling for make-out sessions and drunken hookups with fellow housemates. The good, bad, and ugly of the Shore is what you live for during the summer, but try to stop renting houses with friends once you turn thirty . . . after that it's just tacky.

> **PAISANO Says**
>
> **Tony Soprano:** I think it's time for you to start to seriously consider salads.
> **Bobby Baccalieri:** What do you mean?
> **Tony Soprano:** What do I mean? I mean get off my car before you flip it over, you fat fuck.

DO YOU SPEAK MAFIA?

Any true Guido needs to know his Mafiaese. Between the Godfather trilogy, countless Mafia movies, and The Sopranos, how can you not speak Mafiaspeak in this country? We made up our own humorous definitions; see if you can match the word or phrase with its meaning. Fill in the blanks with the corresponding number.

1. Consigliere

2. Goomara (pronounced like *gumada*)

3. Friend of ours

4. Cugine

5. Vig

6. Omertà

7. Going to mattresses

8. Capo

9. To whack

10. The Boss

11. The joint

12. Zips

13. Box of ziti

14. Gavone

15. Cosa Nostra

16. Pinched

_____ **A.** The interest payment on a loan from a loan shark; what you better cough up by Tuesday or a friend of theirs will show up at your door

_____ **B.** A fat cat who earns his bucks on the backs of his foot soldiers

_____ **C.** Where the wife spends her Sundays sneaking in sausage and coded messages from the Boss

_____**D.** "This thing of ours," which encompasses everyone from the foot soldier to the Boss

_____**E.** An illicit playmate, that is, the woman who didn't give birth to his children and who's really more appropriate for sexual misadventures, like he should bother the wife

_____**F.** A Guido, a young tough guy, wearing a heavy gold chain with greased-back hair trying really hard to become a friend of theirs; dreams of digging graves upstate

_____**G.** If the FBI is listening, last night in the poker game I loaned you a box of ziti (not a grand, you moron)

_____**H.** The suit, except he's in leather and his weapon of choice is a bat rather than a legal brief, and instead of a briefcase full of papers, he has a trunk full of things that need to disappear

_____**I.** The messy slob with pasta dripped all over his wife beater

_____**J.** What happens when the FBI messes up the rug as they drag your husband out of bed and send him packing

_____**K.** Someone who does the same thing you do, that is, he's dug a few graves of his own upstate

_____**L.** Chief whacker, the head of family, has the power to whack

_____**M.** The code of silence or Mafia vow to "do harm and never rat out the family"

_____**N.** Sicilian import brought in to do an "in and out" whack

_____**O.** To eliminate a problem

_____**P.** What happens when rats create a mess or someone insults the boss; going to war with a rival family member, like when one of Tony's capos called Johnny Sacks's wife fat and Johnny started calling up Sealy to place an order

QUIZ ANSWERS

Answers: 1. H; 2. E; 3. K; 4. F; 5. A; 6. M; 7. P; 8. B; 9. O; 10. L; 11. C; 12. N; 13. G. 14. I; 15. D; 16. J

54. You Wear a Diamond-Studded Cross

Gaudy jewelry is in your blood, or at least it seems that way with the atrocious ornaments you've decided to decorate your body with. From earrings to bracelets to watches, everything you wear screams loud and brash. It doesn't matter if you are male or female; the diamond is your best friend. When Jesus died on the cross for you, he didn't mean that he was sacrificing himself on that wooden object so that it could be turned into hundreds of almost identically sized replicas made out of gold and encrusted with diamonds and rubies then worn around the necks of Italians. The tattoo of the cross you got covering your entire back was just not enough for you—you had to get the jewelry to really get your message across. Even if you are blinding to look at directly when out in the sunlight, you love that you're wearing more money than you have in your bank account.

So keep going with the motto "the more diamonds and gold, the better!" and don't ever settle for a piece of jewelry that someone might consider understated.

66 PAISANO Says

Sonny: What's your name, kid?

Calogero "C" Anello: Calogero.

Sonny: That's a long name. Don't you have a nickname?

Calogero "C" Anello: No.

Sonny: What do your friends call you?

Calogero "C" Anello: Calogero.

Sonny: That makes sense. 99

55. You've Created Your Own Fashion Line

If you've taken a shirt that could fit your baby brother, cut three slashes in the front and slapped on a jean skirt that rides just below your crotch, you might think you're the next Coco Chanel. Say you raided your father's closet and stole a couple of silk ties to glue together to make a dress—don't apply to F.I.T. just yet. Owning a pair of scissors and a Bedazzler doesn't make you a fashion designer. J-WOWW said she designed all of the clothes she wore on *Jersey Shore*. Gray sweatpants and a bra is a true fashion statement—it's that whole "homeless chic" thing. And how about that hot yellow number, which was more of a scarf draped across her

> 66 **PAISANO Says**
>
> He goes to talk about his mother. That's what he's doing. He talks about me, he complains. "She didn't do this, she did that." Oh, I gave my life to my children on a silver platter, and this is how he repays me. —**Livia Soprano** 99

braless chest than a "shirt." Now you can buy that priceless gem on her website. Stick to buying your fake Louis Vuittons and Jimmy Choos out of the back of a warehouse in Chinatown and leave the designing to the professionals.

TOUGH-GUY TRIVIA

Bobby Bacala wasn't as fat as he was portrayed on *The Sopranos*. During seasons 2 and 3, the actor, Steve Schirripa, wore a fat suit.

56. Someone in Your Immediate Family Is Named Tony, Gino, Vito, or Isabella

In *Goodfellas*, Karen noted that everyone at her wedding was named Paul, Peter, or Marie. If you were a Guido in the '60s or '70s, that was certainly true. Take a look at your family now. Chances are your brothers are either Tonys, Ginos, or Vitos (with an occassional Paulie thrown in), and you or your sister are Isabellas (but not necessarily Bellas). If, for some reason, your parents named you all after older family members, you're planning on naming your child one of the "Guido four" above. Since there are so many of the same names in the family,

you'll have to come up with a clever way to get the attention of the right person when you shout across the living room.

"Hey, Vito Meatball?"

"Did you call me, Dad?"

"No, I said Vito Meatball, not Vito Calzone, you stunad."

Things might be a bit confusing at first, but you'll figure it out. It's a time-honored tradition to only use a handful of names in the same family.

57. You Hold Your Fork or Spoon Like a Caveman

Handed down through the generations, the art of holding your utensils like a caveman, or an uncultured moron for lack of a better term, is as common to the Italian male as the white tank top and gold chain combination. No matter how important the meal, whether it is the casual Sunday night ritual with the entire, and I mean entire family, or Easter dinner at your mother's house, you hold that fork and knife in your fists with the sharp ends pointing straight up in the air. God forbid you were to sneeze or be pushed forward while sitting at the dinner table! For whatever reason, ever since you were young and you watched your old man eating dinner, you have adopted the art of shoveling food into

❝ PAISANO Says

Paulie Walnuts: Purgatory, a little detour on the way to paradise.

Christopher Moltisanti: How long you think we gotta stay there?

Paulie Walnuts: That's different for everybody. You add up all your mortal sins, multiply that number by fifty, then you add up all your venial sins and multiply that by twenty-five. You add them together, and that's your sentence. I figure I'm gonna have to do about 6,000 years before I get accepted into heaven. And 6,000 years is nothing in eternity terms. I could do that standing on my head. It's like a couple of days here. ❞

your mouth using your spoon like a small spade to devour lasagna at a breakneck speed. Just make sure that one day, when you have a little

goombah of your own, you show him the eating habits of the modern Italian caveman.

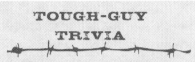

58. You Wear a Pinkie Ring

Showy jewelry has become an element of what you represent as a Guido—and no part of you that is capable of wearing gold or diamonds of some sort should be naked. You started with an extravagant jewel-encrusted silver band on your ring finger, and from there it all went downhill. Next was the thumb and pointer finger, making it nearly impossible to type on a keyboard or pick up small items. Then you took it to the next level and put a rock on your index finger, making the spaces between your fingers even larger. At this point, you figured that it would be doing a disservice to your hand if you left one finger out of the party, so you threw a

> **PAISANO Says**
> **Christopher Moltisanti:** Louis Brazzi sleeps with the fishes.
> **Big Pussy Bonpensiero:** Luca Brasi. Luca . . .
> **Christopher Moltisanti:** Whatever.

"reserved" gold band with diamond inlays on your pinkie, just to complete the set more than anything else. As you get older, maybe you will take one off at a time, slowly "retiring" them into the box of Guido jewelry. But chances are you will be rocking that pinkie ring until the day you die.

Guido Wisdom
Dai nemici mi guardo io, dagli amici mi guardi Iddio!
TRANSLATION: I (can) protect myself from my enemies; may God protect me from my friends!

GUIDO MOVIES MINUS MOBSTERS

- *Rocky*
- *Moonstruck*
- *My Cousin Vinny*
- *Saturday Night Fever*
- *Nuovo Cinema Paradiso*
- *Big Night*
- *Il Postino*
- *Staying Alive*
- *Kiss Me Guido*
- *Fatso*

59. You Drive a Souped-Up Honda Civic with Carriage Lights

Maybe you didn't get that BMW you were expecting on your sixteenth birthday, but what you did get was one sweet diamond in the rough: a Honda Civic. After saving for months and buying some chrome 20s to put on there, it's really starting to look legit. You have all the little things squared away, like the Italian flag reflector on the back, the self-applied purple window tint, and every chrome accent they had to offer at the auto store. Your next modification will be a custom paint job by a buddy of yours at the local auto tech school. You've decided on a two-tone job, with arguably the two most stylin' colors you could come up with—hot pink and lime green. After the paint has dried, it will be right onto the "bumpin'" sound system, so no matter where you go you can bring the club with you. Next will be the purple carriage lights you add to the bottom of the car. Every Guido wants his car to look like some sort of spacecraft. With such a hooked-up ride, you are going to look like a king cruising down the Shore, whipping around in your little Honda with the music blaring. Who wouldn't be envious of you?

Guido Wisdom
La madre degli idioti è sempre incinta.
TRANSLATION: The mother of idiots is always pregnant.

IF YOU'RE A GUIDETTE, HOW OFTEN SHOULD YOU CALL YOUR MA?

☐ On holidays, birthdays, anniversaries, Wednesdays

☐ The first thing in the morning

☐ Before you go to bed at night

☐ Whenever someone is mean to you

☐ Whenever someone is especially nice to you

☐ Whenever your boyfriend says something *stunad*

☐ As soon as you hear gossip about anyone in the family

☐ Whenever you're picking out a present for your sainted brother

☐ Whenever your pedicure smudges ten minutes after you leave the nail salon

Answer: If you want to keep peace, of course it's all of the above, and then some.

TOUGH-GUY TRIVIA

Marlon Brando's mouthpiece from *The Godfather* is on display in the American Mueseum of the Moving Image in Queens, New York.

60. You Say "Fuhgeddaboudit" after Every Sentence—Even If It Doesn't Make Sense

This single phrase has become so versatile in your vocabulary that it literally comes into play after almost every sentence, even if it shouldn't. Whether you are trying to explain to someone that you don't want to do something, or that they shouldn't be worrying about something, or if you just want to hear yourself saying the phrase, you use this phrase in any and every context. While the rest of America simply says "forget about it," you have turned this three-word expression into a slur of five syllables that almost defines a culture. Depending on your tone of voice, you can throw this out as an angry comeback or as a friendly gesture. It would not be inconceivable to find yourself walking by a group of older Italians sitting outside the deli somehow holding a conversation that consisted of nothing more than this simple phrase, but it takes a veteran Guido with a trained ear to decipher.

TOUGH-GUY TRIVIA

Season 5 of *The Sopranos* introduced the arrival of Tony's cousin, named Tony Blundetto. To distinguish them when they were little, neighborhood kids would yell "Tony Uncle Johnny" for Soprano and "Tony Uncle Al" for Blundetto.

GUESS THAT GANGSTER #6

Long before the movies *Analyze This* and *Analyze That* and the TV series *The Sopranos*, this Mafioso was a rare bird among members of the Commission—he was a patient of a psychiatrist. He was also one of the most politically connected members of the syndicate. He had numerous elected officials and judges in his pocket. They were paid well and deeply indebted to him. He is credited with keeping J. Edgar Hoover off the Mafia's case by giving him tips on the horses. And when he gave you a tip, you could be sure it was a sure thing. He was nicknamed Prime Minister of the Underworld because of his skills as a politician and diplomat. He preferred to use nonviolent means to achieve his ends, but like all Mafiosi, violence was a part of his arsenal. He was shot in the head but survived the botched hit and lived to enjoy a comfortable retirement. (See back of the book for the answer.)

61. All of Your "Nice" Clothes Have Animal Prints

You're all dressed up in your Sunday best ready for a night on the town. Unfortunately for you, that means you're wearing at least one article of clothing with an animal print. You've learned the rules of fashion from watching your mom dress up before her night out, and she passed down all of her animal-print tips to you so you could follow in her high-fashion footsteps. You may have even inherited some of her vintage wear from the '70s. You think nothing's hotter than a pair or leopard-spotted vinyl pants or a see-through blouse with tiger stripes. You also own about twenty animal-print thongs with matching bras. On more than one occasion you've walked out of the house wearing two prints that weren't even from the same animal, which is a crime in itself. It's time to throw out those faux-alligator boots and matching wallet and leave the animals at the zoo.

WHAT'S THAT MACARONI?

If you're a real Guido, you call all pasta macaroni. But your Mamma knows there are hundreds of different shapes for pasta. Match the name of the pasta with its shape.

1.	Acini di pepe	A.	Ribbons
2.	Cavatelli	B.	Little wheels
3.	Gemilli	C.	Peppercorns
4.	Rotelle	D.	Hot dog buns
5.	Fusilli	E.	Tiny rings
6.	Penne	F.	Angel hair
7.	Vermicelli	G.	Bow ties
8.	Capellini	H.	Hollow straw
9.	Farfalle	I.	Bells
10.	Bucatini	J.	Small hat
11.	Anellini	K.	Corkscrews
12.	Rocchetti	L.	Little thimbles
13.	Campanelle	M.	Long twists
14.	Rigatoni	N.	Double helix
15.	Cappelletti	O.	Little ears
16.	Ditalini	P.	Quills
17.	Rotini	Q.	Grooved tubes
18.	Papperdelle	R.	Spools
19.	Orecchiette	S.	Spirals
20.	Cavatappi	T.	Little worms

QUIZ ANSWERS

Answers: 1: C; 2: D; 3: N; 4: B; 5: M; 6: P; 7: T; 8: F; 9: G; 10: H; 11: E; 12: R; 13: I; 14: Q; 15: J; 16: L; 17: S; 18: A; 19: O; 20: K

GUESS THAT GANGSTER #7

Nicknamed The Cigar because of the ubiquitous stogie in his mouth, he was by all accounts one of the scariest of a very scary fraternity. He was head of the Bonanno crime family for a while, but he was a dangerous and unstable loose cannon. The Commission unanimously voted to whack him. When he was shot to death in a New York City restaurant, his cigar stayed fixed in his mouth during the shooting and remained between his lifeless lips. (See back of the book for the answer.)

62. You've Blown Your Whole Paycheck at the Track

What Guido doesn't love the track? You go down there with all the degenerates, watch the greyhounds or the horses run from the grandstands, and if you're lucky you grab a sausage and peppers before you leave. Something about being there just makes you feel like a high roller, and as you look up into the glass-covered box seats where the people that can actually afford to be throwing away their money sit, you put yourself into their shoes and act as if you are a true-life gangster. Thankfully, your parents do not make you pay them rent to (still!) live under their roof, so the fact that you just went through your entire paycheck betting on simulcasts and Keno doesn't matter nearly as much as it would if you actually had any bills to pay aside from insurance for your sweet ride. Better luck next time, right?

> ** PAISANO Says**
>
> I'm in the waste management business. Everybody immediately assumes you're mobbed up. It's a stereotype, and it's offensive.
> —**Tony Soprano**

JERSEY SHORE SOUNDBITE

I'm the sweetest bitch you'll ever meet. —SAMMI

63. You Describe Your Dream Guy as a Juicehead

You might not know that a juicehead is someone who uses steroids, you just know that it means the guy has big muscles and that's what you want—some gorilla of a man that can whip you around on the dance floor and carry you on his back when you're too drunk to walk home from the club. You need a guy who's going to protect you from all of the chooches out there who don't show you any respect. Every Guidette wants a bulldog to rescue her, and that's a juicehead. Who doesn't love bulging muscles full of veins and guys with a bit too much testosterone running through them. He's prob-

> 66 **PAISANO Says**
>
> Those who want respect, give respect. —**Tony Soprano** 77

ably sweating more than usual, right? It takes a lot of energy to keep a tank like that running. Just remember to find out if he really is hittin' the juice. A muscled man with a shrunken sack isn't the guy of your dreams.

JERSEY SHORE SOUNDBITE

My ideal man would be Italian, dark, muscles, juicehead, Guido.
—**SNOOKI**

64. You've Walked Home in Tears Without Shoes on More Times Than You Can Count

It's a typical Saturday night (or should we say early Sunday morning.) You've had too many shots of tequila, your boyfriend is acting like a jackass and rubbing his crotch against some bimbo slut, and your girl-friends have already gone home with their chosen Guido of the night. So you gather up your things, make a quick trip to the ladies to puke, take your five-inch stilettos off, and start your tear-filled walk back to your Shore house. Chances of you finding your way back to the house are slim to none. All of the streets look the same at three in the morning. Maybe you can pray

 **PAISANO Says**

There's an old Italian saying: You fuck up once, you lose two teeth.
—**Tony Soprano**

for some cop to take pity on you and give you a ride home—without writing you a ticket for public intoxication.

Guido Wisdom
Chi trova un amico, trova un tesoro.
TRANSLATION: He who finds a friend finds a treasure.

65. You've Received an Italian Horn as a Communion, Birthday, and Graduation Present

The Italian horn (or cornicello) is the ultimate gift for every Guido's first communion, birthday, and graduation. It doesn't matter if you've received one for every national holiday, your aunt Antonia will continue to buy them for you until the day you die. You could never find it in your heart to tell her you already have one . . . or twenty. You have so many of them you could make a charm bracelet (and you probably have.) You have one in gold, one in silver, and one that is diamond encrusted. Originally the Italian horn was used as protection against the evil eye. Since you don't really believe in curses (even though your Ma still does), you just see it as a symbol of your proud heritage. You might have even gotten a tattoo of an Italian horn. It's placed right next to the Italian flag and the red heart that says "Ma."

WISE GUY WISECRACKS
Q. How come Italians don't like Jehovah's Witnesses?
A. They don't like any witnesses

JERSEY SHORE SOUNDBITE

Pauly pulled out his DJ equipment. He's got the Italian thing on the equipment, he has another Italian flag on his book bag, another Italian flag on his laptop. He's the ultimate Guido, he really is.
—RONNIE

66. You're Obsessed with ChapStick or Lip Gloss

There's no excuse to have dry, wrinkled, raisin lips. Sure, your lips might be completely shriveled from the hours spent tanning, but walking out of the house without your ChapStick or lip gloss is not acceptable. You keep a tube in your glove compartment, your nightstand drawer, and one in each pocket of your jeans. You have to be kissably smooth at every second of the day. You never know when you're gonna plant one on some hot guy or girl. Even in the summer it seems your lips are always dry and cracked because you're constantly reapplying. You try to do it in private so it's like your lips are just magically silky smooth. You even have a few tricks up your sleeve to reapply without anyone knowing what you're doing. For some reason it's perfectly fine for a Guido to apply ChapStick when he's outside of the confines of his bathroom. Most people would say there's nothing macho about a guy who whips out the stick and lathers it on, but do you care? No way, guy! Pass the chap and pucker up.

> ❝ **PAISANO Says**
>
> If you can quote the rules, then you can obey them. —**Tony Soprano** ❞

JERSEY SHORE SOUNDBITE 📢

Saturday night, I'm going to Headliners. I'm looking to have more of a classy night tonight. —**VINNIE**

67. Your Ma Throws Holy Water on You When You Come Back from a Date

Oh Ma—God love her, but her prayers and devout commitment to the Lord interfere with your life, especially when it comes to the dating world. No girl is good enough for her "precious," and no punk is coming close to her "princess." You are not even allowed to have a girl down in the basement with you, because she "never did that when she was younger."

It should be all about the romance between an Italian man and woman, and the loving can wait until marriage. Ma never made this clearer than that time you came home past curfew after going on a date

PAISANO Says

A wrong decision is better than indecision. —**Tony Soprano**

with the new girl you met and she doused you with holy water she gets from the priest as soon as you walked through the door. She said she did not want to hear a word of what happened, and you must go to confession this Sunday and ask for the Lord to forgive all of what you may have done inside the movie theater with that little goomah. Now does that not sound like young romance?! If she thinks a little kiss in the theater will send you to hell, don't let her find out what happened on the family couch last night.

JERSEY SHORE SOUNDBITE

I am like a praying mantis. After I have sex with a guy I will rip their heads off. —J-WOWW

68. Your Family Invites Your Priest to Family Functions

It's a big family event, and, once again, your family's priest has been invited. This isn't necessarily a religious occasion like a baptism or first communion; he's here for all the events—birthdays, anniversaries, showers, and Sunday dinner. You even saw his car at your folks' house when you drove by last Tuesday night! Either he doesn't know how to feed himself, or your parents are having marital problems and are getting counseled by the man of the cloth. You don't know how he gets invited, but he always does. Not that you don't appreciate a little blessing on the special day, but it means you have to be on your best behavior. Don't think about showing up drunk from the night before or bringing over some questionable skank you picked up last night. You have enough guilt as a Catholic already! You don't need Father to notice how many sins you are committing at every turn.

 PAISANO Says

Fear knocked on the door. Faith answered. There was no one there.

—**Christopher Moltisanti**

Guido Wisdom
Chi troppo vuole, nulla stringe.
TRANSLATION: He who wants too much doesn't catch anything.

69. You're Obsessed with Drinking Protein Shakes, and You'll Add the Powder to Anything You Can

Thank Jesus for GNC. Building muscle mass has become part of your daily routine, and you obsess about it all the time. Your motivation comes from knowing that when the summer comes, you will be king juicehead down the Shore and the orange midgets will come flocking to you without having to say a word. You hit the gym for five hours a day, but that is not enough. You need "enhancement" help—and protein shakes are just the way to do it! But you don't stop at the simple eight-ounce vanilla crème–flavored shake at the end of your workout; you've implemented protein powder into everything you drink. A nice big glass of whole milk goes great with your ma's spaghetti and meatballs—and apparently now that milk goes great with two scoops of protein. You crack open a can of Coke to wash down the slice you are eating, and somehow manage to choke down what has now become a chocolate fudge Coke protein shake. Making everything you drink into a shake will pay off though, and when you have to buy the next size up in tank tops, you will know you are doing something right.

JERSEY SHORE SOUNDBITE

If you want to look somewhat like The Situation, which is gonna be pretty hard, you need to get that protein in your diet. —THE SITUATION

70. Your Ideal Car Is a Cadillac Escalade with Chrome Wheels That Spin

You've had chrome wheels on your car since you turned sixteen and threw a pair of fake chrome hubcaps from Walmart on your Civic, but now that you are older and you have a bit more money, the car and the chrome have become more extravagant. After the Civic you stepped up to an older-model BMW, which you saved up for, and purchased a nice set of 18-inch chrome rims that you bought off some kid who more than likely stole them, but that just added "street cred" to your ride. Soon after, you got a big Tahoe, to feel like the king Soprano himself, and with that you were able to get the 20s you'd been dreaming about. The only thing left to do now is go for the holy grail of the Guido car kingdom—the Cadillac Escalade with chrome 22s that spin. You would be the coolest cat on the Shore driving something like that, but the money for a Cadillac and those obnoxiously large rims is not going to come easy. Maybe you should follow in the footsteps of your idol Tony Montana and start pedaling drugs to come up with the extra loot. Keep chasing your dreams, Guido. Acquiring things like chrome rims and big cars are admirable goals in life.

> **PAISANO Says**
>
> Even a broken clock is right twice a day. —**Tony Soprano**

WHICH MEMBER OF THE SOPRANO FAMILY ARE YOU?

Even though Tony makes his fortune by committing crimes, you'd love to be a part of the Soprano clan. They live in the lap of luxury, and Carmela cooks dinner every night. Take the quiz below to find out which member you would be.

1. Your favorite thing to do on the weekend is:

A. Go to the country club to play some golf, swing by my favorite strip club, then come home to watch the History Channel with a large bowl of ice cream.

B. Plan the meal for Sunday dinner, clean the kitchen, organize the basement, and meet the girls for lunch at our favorite restaurant to complain about our husbands.

C. Play video games all day, order pizza, have some friends over, and look at porn.

D. Talk politics with my friends from college, try Ecstasy, talk on the phone for hours and complain about my parents.

2. For Christmas, you've asked for:

A. A Big-Mouth Billy Bass

B. A very large sapphire ring

C. Playstation 3

D. Permission to go to Aspen with my friends

3. Your favorite thing to eat is:

A. A bowl of cold spaghetti or cold cuts straight from the refrigerator

B. String beans and mozzerella

C. Pizza

D. Primavera

4. Your biggest pet peeve is:

A. When your wife buys orange juice with pulp in it when you just want "some pulp."

B. When your husband sleeps with anything that has a pulse, including his mother's nurse who has one leg.

C. Being asked to clean the gutters when you don't know what gutters are.

D. When your parents break up a party you've thrown at your grandmother's house.

5. Your favorite Frank Sinatra song is:

A. "My Way"

B. "Almost Like Being in Love"

C. "Glad to Be Unhappy"

D. "High Hopes"

QUIZ ANSWERS

If you had mostly As, you are Tony Soprano. You are the man of the house. What you say goes, at least it does unless your wife stops speaking to you until you change your mind. You have many friends but that might be because they are really afraid of you. Sometimes you feel like you're all alone in the world, and you've been known to go through bouts of depression. It's tough being on top all the time. You enjoy the good times—cooking outside on the grill, playing golf, fishing, smoking a good cigar. You can be self-centered and you often think you deserve everything you want. Sometimes it's hard for you to show emotion without blowing it out of proportion.

If you had mostly Bs, you are Carmela Soprano. You live to serve your family, although secretly you'd like to be a businesswoman (if only you had your own money). You're happy to make wonderful food and keep a clean house, but you often wonder if there's more to life. You turn a blind eye to your husband's indiscretions, but that's getting harder and harder to do. You think that your kids take you for granted and don't respect you. The only fun you have is when you're gossiping with your girlfriends over lunch or flirting with the man who's painting your dining room.

If you had mostly Cs, you are A. J. Soprano. You get everything you ask for and even things you don't. You're spoiled and don't have many boundaries. If you mess up at school, you only get grounded for the weekend, but that means you can still use the computer. Your mom cooks and cleans for you and you have no real responsibility. You want to make your father proud of you so you take an interest in what he likes to do. You have a hard time communicating your feelings, which could prove to be a problem later on.

If you had mostly Ds, you are Meadow Soprano. You are an Italian princess in every sense of the word. Your parents think you can do no wrong, and even when you do screw up, you know how to manipulate the situation to further your own interests. You're a pseudo-intellectual who likes to flaunt the fact that you know more than your parents (who never went to college). Deep down, you still expect them to do everything for you, like clean your clothes when you come home for the weekend and make you a sandwich while you lie by the pool.

71. Instead of a Teething Ring, Your Ma Gave You Biscotti

Growing up in a Guido household, you learned not to waste a thing. Have you ever noticed your mom will reheat coffee that's been left in the coffeepot instead of just making a new cup? You also learned how to be resourceful. Why go out and buy plastic teething rings for your toddler when biscotti work perfectly well? This delicious treat is usually served with a nice cappuccino or espresso, but they're also perfect at soothing a kid's sore mouth. They're so hard that toddlers can gum them all day long. It's too big for a child to choke on, and they just get mushy when soggy, so the pieces that break off are easy to swallow. Show up at any playgroup in a predominantly Italian neighborhood and you'll see that biscotti are the hot new parenting item. Share your family secrets with those not in the know. Buy a box of biscotti as a gift for your next baby shower.

JERSEY SHORE SOUNDBITE

Guidos . . . when we stop, our chrome keeps spinnin. —**PAULY D**

72. You Think That When It Comes to Shorts, the Shorter the Better

As soon as Memorial Day hits, you break out the booty shorts. These are basically underwear with a zipper and back pockets. You have a pair in every color of the rainbow, and you wear them with stilettos so it looks like your legs go on for days. Unlike most girls, you're not embarrassed when it comes to having a "camel-toe" situation. In fact, you're convinced that it really turns the Guidos on, so if you can hike them up even further, great. Let's not leave anything to the imagination. Sometimes you have trouble getting in and out of your short shorts, so when you hit up the bathroom, you can always count on your girls to give you a hand. One of them always has a pair of pliers in her purse to handle a jammed zipper. Even if you have to grease yourself up to get into them, you plan on wearing those shorts until the first frost of the season.

JERSEY SHORE SOUNDBITE

Never fall in love at the Jersey Shore. —RONNIE

73. Despite the Tanning Salons and Your Natural Olive Skin, You Still Use Bronzer

You don't want anyone mistaking your heritage. If they don't know you're Italian, they will once they stand close enough to you to see that layer of thick brown makeup caked onto your face. In your opinion, you can't be too tan looking. In the dead of winter you need to look like you spent a week at the Earth's equator. Even though you spend twenty minutes a day, every day, at the tanning salon, you use a lot of bronzer. You buy three or four compacts of it at a time so you know you always have some on hand. You even buy shades that are three times darker than your natural skin tone. You don't care if you begin to look as orange as a carrot. At least you aren't pasty white! 'Cause that would be the worst thing in the world, right? You spread bronzer on places other than your face as well. Hello. No one wants to see a white ass!

74. You Wear Sunglasses at Night

Corey Hart had it right, but he was from Canada—the land that Guidos forgot. You rocking a pair of Dolce & Gabbana sunglasses at night at the club just makes you look like you are mentally unstable—or are in fact blind. You have become rather accustomed to not being able to see much of anything once the sun sets, and to you it's totally worth it because that way you look "smooth" 24/7. Your favorite line has to be when the girls come over to you and ask to wear your "sick shades" and you get to turn them down, warning them it would be risky to make direct eye contact with you. At least a dozen times you can attribute getting laid with the simple fact that you had your sunglasses on. No matter how good all this is, the best part is that now you can easily hide the black eye you got last night from the juicehead whose girl you decided to hit on.

Guido Wisdom
Chi si volta, e chi si gira, sempre a casa va finire.
IDIOMATIC TRANSLATION: No matter where you go, your house
is always there waiting.

YOU THINK YOU KNOW *THE GODFATHER?*

You wish Vito Corleone was your own dad and that you grew up with the Corleone boys as brothers. You would never have turned against the family like Fredo did. Stupid idiot. Think you know *The Godfather* by heart? Take the quiz and find out.

1. After work Vito decides he wants to buy something before going home. If he hadn't stopped he probably wouldn't have been gunned down. What was Vito buying when he was shot?

A. A toy truck

B. Fruit

C. The newspaper

D. A new car

2. Vito is playing with his grandson on the day that he dies. What type of citrus does Vito put into his mouth to scare his grandson in the garden?

A. An orange

B. A lime

C. A lemon

D. A grapefruit

3. Michael is trying to call Luca Brasi when a package arrives at the Corleone home. It is a package wrapped in newspaper that is to be taken as a Sicilian message that Luca is dead. What is wrapped in the newspaper?

A. A pizza

B. Dry pasta

C. A leg of lamb

D. Fish

4. Johnny Fontane is at the end of his rope when he shows up at Connie's wedding to surprise her with a song. When Vito is giving Johnny Fontane some advice, he tells him that a he can never be a real man unless he:

A. Has a gold record

B. Spends time with his family

C. Drives a Cadillac

D. Kills a man

5. Vito and the family turn down an offer from the Sollozzo to get into a questionable business. What did he want him to be involved in trafficking?

A. Stolen items

B. Guns

C. Drugs

D. Prostitutes

6. What holiday was approaching when Vito got shot?

A. Christmas

B. Thanksgiving

C. Halloween

D. Easter

7. Who comes to visit Vito in the hospital while Michael is there?

A. Sonny

B. Vinny

C. Guiseppe

D. Enzo

8. Tom Hagen was adopted by the Corleone family when he was a kid. He does not have Sicilian blood. What nationality is he?

A. French

B. Polish

C. German Irish

D. Native American

9. After killing McCluskey and Sollozzo, Michael flees to Sicily to avoid persecution. While in Sicily he meets a girl and marries her. What is her name?

A. Angelina

B. Appolonia

C. Amelia

D. Adria

10. Michael's enemies know he is in Sicily and arrange for his wife to be killed. How does she die?

A. Michael kills her in her sleep

B. She drowns in a lake

C. The car she is driving blows up

D. She dies in her sleep

11. The plan is set for Michael to take revenge on McCluskey and Sollozzo. Tessio finds the perfect restaurant for him to make the hit. What is the name of the restaurant?

A. Louis'

B. Luigi's

C. Lorenzo's

D. Larry's

12. Before they send Michael off to kill McCluskey and Sollozzo, the gang sits down for a takeout dinner. What did they order?

A. Indian

B. Sub sandwiches

C. Pizza

D. Chinese

13. On orders from Michael Corleone, a hitman murders Moe Green? How does Moe Green get killed?

A. Decapitated

B. Shot in the eye

C. Strangled to death

D. Poisoned

14. After he does nothing to save his father from being murdered, Fredo is sent away to learn a new business. Where is he sent?

A. Reno

B. Los Angeles

C. Las Vegas

D. Orlando

15. Even though Tom Hagen isn't related by blood, the family trusts him as an important member of the family business. What is his profession?

A. Lawyer

B. Gardener

C. Doctor

D. Accountant

16. Sollozzo is desperate to get the Corleone in on his business. He has a unique nickname. What is it?

A. The Cannoli

B. The Espresso

C. The Turk

D. The Russian

17. One of Don Vito Corleone's enforcers, the bumbling Luca Brasi meets his ultimate demise at the Tattaglia restaurant. How is he killed?

A. Thrown off a bridge

B. Strangled with wire

C. Wine is poisoned

D. Shot in the head

18. Fat Clemenza hides a gun in the restaurant where Michael kills McCluskey and Sollozzo. Where is the gun hidden?

A. Under a table

B. In a bowl of spaghetti

C. Behind a radiator

D. Behind an old-fashioned toilet

19. At the beginning of the movie, Vito is meeting with anyone who wants to ask for his help on the day of his daughter's wedding. He is playing with one of his pets at the time. What kind of animal is it?

A. A cat

B. A dog

C. A bird

D. A turtle

20. What is the name of Don Vito's consigliere before Tom takes his place?

A. Gino

B. Genco

C. Georgie

D. Gill

QUIZ ANSWERS

Answers: 1: B; 2: A; 3: D; 4: B; 5: C; 6: A; 7: D; 8: C; 9: B; 10: C; 11: A; 12: D; 13: B; 14: C; 15: A; 16: C; 17: B; 18: D; 19: A; 20: B

75. You Start Getting Ready at 7 to Go Out at 11.

It's seven o'clock at night and you have four hours until you head to the club. Your girls and/or guys have shown up early for a little pregame boozing. You turn on some jams and hit the shower. Your shower routine takes about an hour, and you're lucky if the water stays hot that long. Hey, it takes a long time to remove all of the hair on your body and make sure you smell fresh and clean. Next it's onto the hair on your head. That's a task in itself and can easily take up to an hour. Makeup application is a skill that requires your undivided attention. Start with concealer, base, and bronzer. Add fake eyelashes with a thick line of liquid eyeliner and top it off with a hefty coat of ruby red lipstick and you look like you're getting ready to go on stage for a production of *Rocky Horror Picture Show*. Last, but certainly not least, is your wardrobe. You don't put much thought into this as you don't plan on wearing it for very long. Do a shot of Jack, grab your purse, and you and your friends are out the door for a three-hour night of debauchery—less time than it took to get prepped! That's time management, Guido style.

JERSEY SHORE SOUNDBITE

I wait till the last minute to shave. I wait till the last minute to put the shirt on 'cause you feel fresh. These are rules to live by: shave last minute, haircut the day of, maybe some tanning and the gym. You gotta do the Guido handbook. —THE SITUATION

76. You Think Rosary Beads Are a Fashion Statement, Not a Method of Prayer

Remember when your grandmother gave you rosary beads for your first communion? She expected you to pray to the Virgin Mary every night before bed, but you've decided to wear them as a fashion statement. Many people first saw Madonna wearing rosary beads during her "Like a Virgin" days. That was when she still had a little Guidette in her. You started wearing them around your neck at the age of thirteen, just around the time you started questioning your faith (but don't tell your folks that). They seemed trendy and cool, and as soon as you started wearing them, your friends did the same. Your Ma would give you a smack in the head and bless herself when you wore them to the dinner table as if you had come to the table with devil horns on your head. To this day, you still think they are the perfect addition to any animal-print dress.

Guido Wisdom
Chi parla in faccia non è traditore.
TRANSLATION: He who speaks to your face is not a traitor.

77. You've Never Actually Been to Italy (and You Call It the Other Side)

You've heard all the stories about the Other Side, but most of what you believe and know about Italy you pieced together from TV and the movies. You cannot pronounce the last name of your ancestors, or even the town that they came from, but you pretend you know how it's pronounced when you're out talking to friends and ladies and the subject of your heritage comes up. You even throw in an Italian word or two to really make it seem like the separation between you and the homeland you've never even visited is only a mere body of water. If anyone asks, you go there every summer to stay in your family's summer house, but that could not be further from the truth. If it was not for the gold Italian horn around your neck and the smell of veal Parmesan coming off your velour track suit, no one would even know you were of Italian descent. So keep reusing words that you hear constantly on *The Sopranos* and no one will be the wiser as to the fact that you have never stepped foot outside of New Jersey.

WHAT IS YOUR *JERSEY SHORE* NICKNAME?

Every Guido needs a cool nickname, like The Situation. How do you expect people to take you seriously unless you have a serious nickname? Take this short quiz to find out what you would be called down at the Shore. Consider tattooing it onto your biceps, or, at the very least, get it ironed onto a pair of underwear.

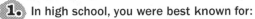 **In high school, you were best known for:**

A. Hanging around the popular kids and doing everything they did so they would think you were cool.

B. Falling in love with every boy or girl who talked to you—even if it was just to ask to borrow your pen.

C. Picking fights with the younger, more fashion-challenged group of kids—because you thought you were better than them.

D. Being a loner. You never hung out with a group of people, but you might have been attached at the hip to one friend. You always had your nose in a book.

E. Getting all of your homework in on time. You studied hard and didn't fool around. You never went to weekend parties and preferred to study for the SATs.

2. **If your boss talked about your reputation at work, he would say:**

A. You are up his ass every five seconds trying to see if there is anything you can do to be as successful as him.

B. You fall all over the other employees and even flirt with the customers on a regular basis. You're constantly giving off the vibe that you are looking for love.

C. You have a hard time getting along with your coworkers and have a real problem with authority. The managers don't want you to work on their shift so they draw straws when making up your schedule for the week.

D. You keep to yourself and aren't overly friendly with customers or coworkers. You do what's asked of you, but no more.

E. You arrive early to work and stay late. You take on more than you need to and don't joke around. Some may say you don't have a sense of humor, and you might make other coworkers nervous. You're not a manager, but you act like one.

3. Everyone knows you at the club, but that's not always a good thing. They know your persona before they know your name. People have said:

A. "She wore the same thing that I was wearing that night and looked like complete trash. Girl needs to get her own style."

B. "He proposed after two dances and three margaritas. He told me I was the love of his life. I just ran as fast as I could."

C. "I accidentally bumped into him on the way to the bathroom and he told me he would pound me into oblivion. I'm afraid for my life."

D. "She shows up and orders a wine cooler. She drinks half of it and stands in the corner all night. No one asks her to dance because she looks like she might cry if you do."

E. "He's the designated driver. He always acts like the parent and makes sure his friends stay in line and no one gets too sloppy. You can count on him to take care of you, but sometimes he just needs to lighten up."

QUIZ ANSWERS

If you had mostly As, you are The Replication. You have no style of your own and you're a basic wannabe. You've been this way since high school and are desperate to be in the cool group. Your boss is tired of you brownnosing, and if you wear someone else's designer outfit to the club, you're going to get a smack. Try and find yourself and forget what everyone else thinks.

If you had mostly Bs, you are The Infatuation. The only thing you have on your mind is falling in love. It's your main goal in life, and in a world full of hookups, it's not working out too well. People aren't looking for anything serious right now, so when you propose marriage after two dances at the club, people run for the door. If you really want to find true love, stay out of the clubs. And for god sakes, don't act so desperate!

If you had mostly Cs, you are The Instigation. You're pissed and you don't even know why. One wrong look from another Guido and you are charging after him like a bull. People are actually afraid of you and can't deal with your unpredictable behavior. Your friends can't deal with your tantrums any longer. It might be time for some anger management therapy or you can bet you'll be alone for a very long time.

If you had mostly Ds, you are The Trepidation. You worry too much about everything. You let your fear stand in your way of a good time. You'll never pick up a hot guy or girl if you don't let your guard down a little. Have a shot of tequila and let loose. You only live once.

If you had mostly Es, you are The Regulation. You do things by the book. You are all about law and order, and you can be a bit uptight. You get down to business and have a hard time having fun because of it. Your friends know you will take care of them if they get into trouble, but they would rather see you enjoy yourself.

78. Your Neighborhood Constantly Smells Like Frying Garlic

You head outside to walk your dog, and as soon as you open the door you're hit with a wave of odor that's so familiar and comforting it's like you're a kid again helping your Ma in the kitchen. The overwhelming smell of frying garlic permeates the air and makes your mouth water. You're hungry throughout the entire day. It's not just coming from one house—it's coming from every house. If you live in a predominantly Italian neighborhood, you know exactly what this is like. It's often pleasant, except on Sundays when it's just too much to handle. You know exactly what each neighbor is making for Sunday dinner, and it obviously predominantly features garlic. You have to close your windows and stay inside or the smell will stay in your clothes, skin, and hair for a week. Italians don't ask their neighbors to borrow a cup of milk or sugar, they ask if they can borrow a few cloves of garlic to make Sunday gravy.

GUESS THAT GANGSTER #8

He was the deceptively docile don who became the Boss of Bosses after Lucky Luciano was deported back to Italy. He was originally thought of as a timid and cowardly man. He endured much humiliation from the hot-tempered Albert Anastasia, but he was working behind the scenes to whack his volatile boss and seize control. And when he did, he elevated his crime family into an efficient and profitable enterprise. He was a successful don and died of natural causes in 1976. The power plays that followed his death led to the rise of John Gotti and his reign during the 1980s and early 1990s. (See back of the book for the answer.

79. You Consider Your Friends Part of the Family

To a Guido, nothing is more important than family. That's just something that's ingrained in your head from the time you are a young child. Your family is there for you no matter what, and that's something you don't mess with. However, next in line (after hair gel) are your friends. To you, friends are family. They are invited to family functions, and you still have the same friends you've had since kindergarten. Your folks see them as their own kids and will feed them that way. They don't have to knock on the door when they come over, and they'll even ask your folks for advice. You know they'll always have your back in a brawl or will be there as a shoulder to cry on when that asshole doesn't call the next morning. Great friends are one of the best benefits to being a Guido.

Guido Wisdom
Chi ha la mamma sua non piange mai.
TRANSLATION: He who has his own mother never cries.

80. You Can't Speak Italian but You Can Understand What Your Nonnie Is Saying

Your Nonnie has been in this country since she was a kid, but she still refuses to speak English, especially in her own house. There's a good side and a bad side to this. The good side is that since you were a kid you've been exposed to everything she says, which means you understand Italian, but you can't actually speak it. You would never survive if you ever went to the Other Side. Another thing that can be awkward about Nonnie not speaking a word of English is that it makes your non-Italian-speaking friends paranoid. When they come over for a visit and she is there, they always think that she is talking about them . . . which she probably is.

Guido Wisdom
Chi mangia solo crepa solo.
TRANSLATION: He who eats alone dies alone.

81. You're Still Pissed Off at the Way *The Sopranos* Ended

The Sopranos changed your life, and now you're watching the last fifteen minutes of the series finale, on the edge of your seat biting your nails. The tension is rising and you just know the show is going to end triumphantly. Your hero, Tony, walks into a diner and takes a seat facing the door. He quickly breezes through the menu and flips through the songs at the jukebox. He chooses Journey's "Don't Stop Believing." Carmela walks in as the song starts and sits down. Some suspicious-looking dude in a Member's Only jacket comes in followed by A. J., while Meadow is trying to parallel park her car outside the diner. A. J. talks about "remembering the good times." Meadow is still trying to park. The Member's Only guy walks by the family to go to the bathroom. Meadow finally walks in and the screen turns black. This is when you screamed, "What the f*!#!" and ran to your cable box to wiggle some wires. Then you grabbed the remote and furiously changed the channel to see if there was a problem with the other stations only to realize there was nothing wrong. You slowly sit back on the couch and stare at the rolling credits in disbelief. What the hell just happened? Is Tony dead? Is this a joke? Was that the biggest cop-out in the world? You sat through a final season of crap for a series finale of more crap? After six years of loyalty, there's only one thing to say. Vafanculo, David Chase! You had to avoid all of the radio stations and people talking at work about it the next day or your blood pressure started to rise. Even now, you're breaking out in a mild sweat. And if you hear one more person say they really liked how it ended and it was really artistic, you're going to grab the bat from your trunk and cause a problem. Take a deep breath and just remember that you're not the only one who was disappointed.

A GUIDO'S FASCINATION WITH BURIAL PLOTS

Funerals are huge events for Guidos, and they go all out for their friends and loved ones. When it comes to flowers, they love red, green, or white carnations—sprinkled with glitter. They tend to send an overdone spray or wreath on a stand, very grand. It will often not be an understated arrangement like white lilies. It will probably be way too big and will have a banner that says, "We will miss you, Nonna" in sparkles.

Italian-American headstones almost always have a cross or a carving or sculpture of the Virgin Mary. The whole family will be buried in one area, and the widow or widower goes every week to create a shrine, using stuffed animals, flowers, pictures, or handwritten notes. It becomes her new home.

It's like Italians are obsessed with their own funerals—and the cemetery. Many Italians visit the cemetery all the time, for no reason except maybe to walk their dogs. On all holidays, especially religious ones, they'll blanket their loved ones' graves with flowers, and then they'll also randomly place flowers on someone's grave who died in Vietnam or graves that look like no one comes to visit them.

PIMP MY GRAVESTONE

Italians also love to decorate the other piece of primary real estate they own—the gravesites of their loved ones. See if you can think of at least five items you would typically find on a pimped-out gravesite.

_____

_____

_____

_____

_____

Possible answers: Italian flags that flap in the wind; pictures of them, their children, their grandchildren, their mother; a large lavender cross; rosary beads; Mass cards from the funeral; a shrine honoring what the deceased did in life (fire hat, police cap); a statue of a favorite saint; a blue statue of Mary with her arms upraised; flower arrangements in all shapes, sizes, and colors

82. Your Family Owns Its Own Restaurant—and You Worked There Every Summer of Your Childhood

The family restaurant—it was the pride of Italian cuisine in your hometown. Ma and Pa were the head chefs, your sisters were the main servers, and you got to do the dishes and bus tables. It was your second home every summer—and you hated it. The loving parents you knew would disappear when it came time to run the restaurant, and they would often resemble slave drivers the way they made their children work, but it was to teach you some values and the meaning of a "hard day's work." You decided at a young age that you never wanted to work in the restaurant business again—unless it involved wearing loose-fitting shirts behind the bar while you poured cocktails and had women gazing at you with admiration and lust. Now that you've grown up, the restaurant has closed and is now a pizza place, and your summers are spent on the Shore being a drunken mess—but you will never forget the great times you had single-handedly washing all the manicotti-caked dishes from the Sunday Italian brunch the family served up every week.

83. You Call Your Mom and Dad "Ma" and "Pop"

Like most Italians over the age of forty, they act like they are elderly. It's like one night you're at the club and the next you're in the nursing home. It's a strange phenomenon. So to make their names match their "age," you don't call your Mom and Dad "Mom" and "Dad," you say "Ma" and "Pop."

"Ma, can you bring me another bowl of ziti?"

"Pop, can you help me change the oil in my car?"

You see these two names as terms of endearment, especially as you scream them from down in the basement or out on the front lawn. However, if you're outside and yell "Ma!" about twenty women in the neighborhood yell "What!" back. You love your folks more than anything because they do absolutely everything for you. Get out there and do something nice for them for a change—like move out of their house.

Guido Wisdom
Chi la sera i pasti li ha fatti, sta agli altri lavare i piatti.
TRANSLATION: If one cooks the meal then the others wash up.

GUESS THAT GANGSTER #9

This gangster was the head of his own crime family and another ambitious killer who sought to be the Boss of Bosses. His dubious contribution was to keep the Mafia in the drug business. This was a controversial issue. There was "a lot of money in that white powder," as Sonny Corleone said in *The Godfather*. But the old-timers thought it was a nasty business, dangerous and destructive compared to gambling and prostitution. It was his drug trafficking that got him in trouble with the law, and he died in the slammer, one of the rare instances where a power-seeking don did not get himself whacked by rivals. (See back of the book for the answer.

84. You've Said "I'm Getting Fresh to Death"

You heard Pauly D say it on *Jersey Shore* and now you can't stop repeating this ridiculous phrase. Hygiene is everything to you, so you totally identify with his philosophy. Cleanliness is next to godliness, right? When you go out to the club the last thing you want to be is sweaty and dirty. How you manage to avoid this is a mystery, but you think that by throwing on your shirt as you're walking out the door for the night you're going to be a fresh as a daisy. You have to look like you just stepped out of the tanning bed and the hair salon all at the same time. But, really, you aren't fooling anyone. By the time you've battled on the floor, smoked a few butts, had a few shots, and kissed a couple of girls, your gel will be melting and running down your face, you'll smell like an ashtray, and you've probably contracted oral herpes. There's nothing fresh about that.

JERSEY SHORE SOUNDBITE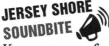

You gotta stay fresh-to-death I call it—fresh outfit, fresh haircut, fresh tan, just stay fresh. —PAULY D

THE GREATEST GUIDO/GUIDETTE ACTORS

- Danny Aiello
- Armand Assante
- Lorraine Bracco
- Steve Buscemi
- Nicholas Cage
- Steve Carell
- Tony Danza
- Robert De Niro
- Danny DeVito
- Vincent D'Onofrio
- Annette Funicello
- James Gandolfini
- Janeane Garofalo
- Anthony LaPaglia
- Susan Lucci
- Madonna
- Alyssa Milano
- Liza Minelli
- Al Pacino
- Chazz Palminteri
- Joe Pantoliano
- Joe Pesci
- Isabella Rossellini
- Rene Russo
- Sylvester Stallone
- Marisa Tomei
- John Travolta
- Stanley Tucci
- John Turturro

85. Your Family Will Disown You If You Don't Marry an Italian

When you were in high school you brought home someone you were dating for dinner. She wasn't Italian, and that's a mistake you'll never make again. Your family usually welcomes your friends with open arms and makes sure they get served first if they stay for dinner. But if you even hint that you like each other more than friends and your mother doesn't know his or her mother from church, fuhgeddaboudit! They'll be kicked out so fast they won't even have time to stuff one of your Mamma's meatballs in their face. Guidos are old-fashioned at heart, and every Guido parent wants to see his little boy settle down with a nice girl who can trace her heritage back to the old country. A mother needs to know her son will be fed well once he gets married (even though no one can cook as well as she can). And every father wants his baby girl to marry a man who knows what it means to treat her like an Italian princess. As archaic as it may seem, do yourself a big favor and stick to your own kind.

JERSEY SHORE SOUNDBITE

My ultimate dream is to move to Jersey; find a nice, juiced, hot, tanned guy; and live my life.—**SNOOKI**

86. You Have No Problem Wearing Animal Fur

Your prized possession is your 100 percent mink fur coat that your boy-friend bought you after only a month of dating. You love it so much, you would wear it in the summer if you could. However, if someone gave you a fake fur coat, you probably couldn't tell the difference. You would die for a pair of alligator boots, and you would shave your cat to make a pair of socks. You have no qualms about wearing animal fur or skin and don't understand why people get so upset about it. When people say to you "What about PETA?" You say, "No thanks, I don't like Middle Eastern food." Way to keep up with current events. We'll chalk it up to naiveté because you probably think the animals died of natural causes—so why let the fur go to waste? Beware of people who throw red paint.

GUESS THAT GANGSTER #10

He was a friend of Frank Sinatra, and he also shared a girlfriend with President John Fitzgerald Kennedy. He was instrumental in using Mafia influence in hopes of helping John F. Kennedy become president but came to quickly regret it when Attorney General Robert Kennedy began an aggressive campaign against the mob. He was also a violent-tempered, murderous hoodlum who was a high-level member of the Chicago crime family. According to one of Shirley MacLaine's many volumes of memoirs, she was at a party with him and his date, whom Shirley described as a "dominatrix." This is an interesting insight into the psychology of a powerful Mafioso. He was a man who inspired fear in the world of the Mafia, but behind closed doors he may have explored his submissive side. Conspiracy theories also link him with the JFK assassination. He was murdered in 1975. (See back of the book for the answer.)

87. You Have No Fewer Than Twenty Cousins and They Were All in Your Wedding

When most people say they have a big family, they usually mean two siblings and a handful of cousins. When you talk about your big family, you have five or six siblings and no fewer than twenty cousins. Ah . . . the joys of growing up a Catholic Italian. You have to rent out a hall just to have a birthday party in your family. When you were planning your wedding, each cousin needed to be included in the wedding party. God forbid you neglect to include a member of the family. No one would recover from that scandal. Your family's not just involved in the wedding, every one of them has an opinion, and you better heed their advice or they will be insulted. You will never hear the end of it. Your photographer needs to use an extra-wide camera lens just to fit everyone in the picture. Chances are you don't need to hire a hair stylist or makeup artist because your cousins Antonia and Marianne just got their licenses from Blaine Beauty School. Sometimes it pays to have a big family.

A TYPICAL GUIDO FAMILY

You know you're Guido if your family is bigger than a football team. Just for fun, see if you can pick out all the members of an Italian family. Select all that apply:

1. Great-grandparents

2. Grandmothers and grandfathers on both sides

3. About fifty-eight aunts and uncles

4. At least ninety-nine cousins

5. Godparents for each child

6. The family doctor

7. The parish priest

8. The neighbors on both sides

9. All of the above

QUIZ ANSWERS

Answer: Of course it's all of the above—and more! Italian families embrace everyone in their orbit, everyone who plays a major, or even a minor, role in their lives on a continuing basis. Italian children often call their parents' friends "aunt" and "uncle," which leads to hordes of "cousins."

88. You Think Scorsese Is God

Martin Marcantonio Luciano Scorsese, or just plain Marty, is the greatest director to ever live. You've seen every movie he's ever made, and when a new one comes out you're first in line on opening day. You've been a fan since you were old enough to watch *Goodfellas*. You acted out the "Funny how?" scene in your bedroom and looked up to Tommy like a big brother. You've seen both *Taxi Driver* and *Raging Bull* starring your idol Bobby about a hundred times each. You've hosted "Marty Parties" where you have a Marty marathon and then discuss the films at length with your friends (who, by the way, are over your obsession). Even his lesser-known films, like *Bringing Out the Dead* and *Kundun*, made you think he could do no wrong. That's dedication and loyalty, my friend. Not only is he Italian, he's an Italian who's an inspiration.

> **PAISANO Says**
>
> When you're married, you'll understand the importance of fresh produce!—**Tony Soprano**

GUESS THAT GANGSTER #11

Nicknamed The Oddfather by the media, this Mafia don had a unique strategy to avoid prosecution. He wandered around his New York City neighborhood in a bathrobe chattering away to himself. He hoped his reputation as mentally ill would enable him to plead insanity in the event he was ever brought to trial. But FBI wiretaps recorded a sane and lucid person on tape. In his youth he shot Frank Costello in the head, though the injury didn't kill Costello. This gangster who could not shoot straight tried to convince the feds that he was a don that could not think straight. He died while in prison custody in 2005. (See back of the book for the answer.)

89. You Didn't Go to College (Unless You Count That Semester and a Half at Community College)

How can you possibly be expected to sit through four years of college when there are so many cooler things you could be doing? You gave it a shot. You went to community college for a semester and a half, but it just cut into your party time. You couldn't figure out how to stay up all night at the club then make it to your 8:00 A.M. Western Civilization class. You didn't see how reading Shakespeare made you smarter than learning some new drink-pouring skills at bartending school or hair-dressing skills at the local beauty school. In your mind, college is all about making connections anyway, and you already have those. Your cousin Christopher can hook you up with a job at his auto body shop, so you're not worried.

TOP TEN OCCUPATIONS FOR A GUIDO
1. Disc jockey
2. Clothing designer
3. Hair dresser
4. Small screen actor
5. Construction worker
6. Firefighter
7. Bartender
8. Car salesman
9. Script writer
10. Mobster

90. You're the King of Breakin' Balls

You're not an asshole. You're not a jerk-off. You're just the king of breakin' balls. You bust 'em like no other—and everyone knows it. Having a conversation with you is a challenge fit for only the toughest characters, because you will pick apart someone until he or she is on the verge of tears. You remember every little embarrassing episode that ever happened to someone, and you do not hesitate to cut into someone by bringing it up. You will laugh off any attempt to have your own balls busted by others and simply retort with a remark

WISE GUY WISECRACKS

Q: *How can you tell if an Italian is in the Mafia?*
A: *His favorite dish is broken leg of lamb*

about their hairstyle, the car they drive, the clothes they have on, or even the name they chose for their first-born. There are simply no lines you will not cross when it comes to breakin' balls—and at this point you have unofficially been anointed the king of doing it. It may have cost you all your friends, but it was worth all the laughs you got out of it.

91. You Have Some Serious Connections

When it comes to getting your laundry done, you get the hangers put on your collared shirts—at no extra charge. When it comes to getting a coffee in the morning—they give you two shots of espresso when you only asked for one. You are also pretty sure that when you got stopped last week for not wearing a seatbelt the cop did not give you a ticket because he must have realized who he was dealing with. You've got all the connections . . . even though you're not connected! You use little "perks" like these all the time when you take girls out to convince them you have the "in" with all the local businesses and government officials. You tell

them you're part of a very important "family," but we all know that the only family you are a part of is the one whose basement you still live in. You can pretend to be a made man all you want, but you swing about as much influential power around as a Taco Bell employee. That reminds me—isn't it about time you went out and got a job?

GUESS THAT GANGSTER #12

Known as the Dapper Don, he was the last of the great flamboyant folk hero Mafiosi. He became the Capone of modern times, but the Teflon Don who had successfully avoided prosecution for many years became the Velcro Don who ended up in the slammer. He became head of the Gambino crime family after orchestrating the murder of Paul Castellano and became a media darling during his years in power. His celebrity status went to his head, and he left himself open for prosecution by his arrogant attitude. He was ultimately betrayed by his underboss, Sammy "The Bull" Gravano, but most agree that it was his hubris and recklessness that did him in. He was sent away for life in 1992. He developed terminal cancer while in prison and died in 2002 at the age of sixty-one. (See back of the book for the answer.)

92. You and Your Family Have Vanity License Plates of Your Last Name

The family garage is packed: two BMWs, one Range Rover, one Tahoe, and the Honda Civic you got stuck with—all with tinted windows and chrome rims, of course. This is not all they have in common, though, as each one has been fitted with a vanity plate featuring the last name of the family and a number one through five. It's a beautiful sight on the weekend when Pop pulls "Giordano #1" and "Giordano #3" out for a clean and a wax. The family also finds

> **PAISANO Says**
>
> *Kundun*. I liked it! —**Christopher Moltisanti yelling at Scorsese**

convenience in this, as they can simply call out, "Hey, leave me #2 'cause I gotta run to the hair salon lata!" You do not know it, but people around the town cannot help but laugh a little when they see your convoy of numbered Guidomobiles zipping around town. That is all right though, because they are clearly just jealous that they would only have to get two plates: "Smith #1" and "Smith #2" . . . and both of them are minivans.

SUPERSTITIOUS GUIDOS

Italians are famously superstitious and often have their own little ways of doing things that they can't fully explain, other than to say, "It's always been done that way in my family." Their little superstitions will affect the way they make even simple decisions. On *The Sopranos*, Uncle Junior picked his doctor because his name was Kennedy, and he loved the Kennedy clan (even though they were Irish Catholics), but it could be the name of anyone they revered. It makes no sense, but it's very common! Here are some common Guido superstitions:

- The evil eye. Caused by jealousy and envy, a person can curse you using the evil eye, causing sickness until the curse is broken.
- Keeping a bird in the house brings bad luck.
- A loaf of bread must always be placed face up or else bad luck will come.
- The number 17 is extremely unlucky.
- A new house has to be blessed before you can move in.
- Never stick a knife into a loaf of bread unless you are cutting it.
- You'll get punished if something good happens to you.
- Never toast with a glass of water.
- You must remember to look someone in the eyes while you are toasting.
- Putting shoes on a counter is bad luck.
- Buying shoes for a newborn baby is good luck.
- Don't spill wine at the dinner table.
- Never cross arms when shaking hands in a group.

GUESS THAT GANGSTER #13

He was John Gotti's underboss and one of the rats who decided to save his own hide and sing to the feds. He confessed to murdering nineteen people over a twenty-year period, an average of about one whack per year. The state thought he would be an invaluable asset in nailing the Teflon Don. His testimony brought down several members of the Gambino, Colombo, and Genovese crime families, including the seemingly indestructible John Gotti. He was granted immunity and entered the Witness Protection Program. He had an active criminal life under his alias while living in Arizona. He is currently in jail on drug charges. (See back of the book for the answer.)

93. Your Current Girlfriend Is a Cougar

You're not one to carry on a serious relationship, but when you do, it's with someone twice your age. You'd never know she was in her mid-forties by looking at her. Hell, you didn't know her age until two months in when you took a peek at her license while she was in the shower. You had your suspicions, but you also figured sitting in the tanning booth just made her skin dry out. Now that you know, you're even more into her. A cougar can give you everything you want—and make some good grub. Sure, it's a little bit like dating your mother, but somehow you can justify it. Your buddies all think you scored big because she probably knows what she's doing in the sack and she probably makes her own money, which means you don't have to pay every time you go out. Every Guido just wants to marry someone like his Mamma anyway, so play on! Just don't mess up because cougars don't have the patience to put up with any Guido bullshit.

> **PAISANO Says**
>
> **Dr. Jennifer Melfi:** What's the one thing every woman—your mother, your wife, your daughter—have in common?
> **Tony Soprano:** They all break my balls.

94. You Think Axe Body Spray Is High-Class Cologne

Every high school student across the country gets out of gym class and plasters on a thick layer of Axe body spray because it is both cheap and potent. This is the only application where such vile "cologne" should be administered. Once you are older than sixteen, you should never again purchase any cologne that is sold at department stores and pharmacies and holds such names as "Phoenix" and "Voodoo." While most people would deem this product worthy of masking the odor of a litter box, the Guido is convinced that such body sprays are the top-of-the-line fragrance for men—and they wear it religiously. With a can on the dresser—and in the glove box of the car, and in the gym locker, and a travel size in their inner jacket pocket—they are ready for a quick blast of spicy mint and citrus death at any occasion. I suppose anything is better than smelling like a sweaty sausage grinder, but who knows, that might be the next aroma the clever folks at Axe come out with.

> **PAISANO Says**
>
> **Jimmy Altieri:** I got enough cologne on?
> **Christopher Moltisanti:** You smell like Paco Rabanne crawled up your ass and died.

GUESS THAT GANGSTER #14

He, along with Meyer Lansky and others, formed the National Syndicate, also known as the Commission. He came out on top in the aftermath of the Castellammarese War, when the old and conservative Mustache Petes were completely ousted from power. He turned the Mafia into a well-organized and profitable corporate-like entity. He was ultimately arrested, only to get an early release because of his contributions to the war effort during World War II. He was exiled to his native Italy where he died in 1962. He did not live a quiet life when deported. He organized an efficient and massive drug empire that smuggled heroin into the United States and created hundreds of thousands of addicts. (See back of the book for the answer.)

95. You Take Christopher Columbus Day Off from Work

Sure, it's a national holiday, but you and your family treat it like it's Christmas. As soon as the new work year starts in January, you're asking your boss for a day off on October 12. The Irish have St. Patrick's Day, while the Italians have Christopher Columbus Day. You see it as a celebration of your heritage. Even though most would agree that Chris did some awful things in his time, Guidos look at him as an icon. You love to brag that an Italian discovered America as if that means you deserve to live here more than any other nationality. You and the family head out to the Columbus Day parade and proudly wave your Italian flags. Then it's back to the house for a large feast. Enjoy the day.

 **PAISANO Says**

> He discovered America is what he did. He was a brave Italian explorer. And in this house, Christopher Columbus is a hero. End of story. —**Tony Soprano**

👑
Guido Wisdom
Amicu ca non ti duna, parendi ca non ti mpresta, fuili comu la pesta.
SICILIAN TRANSLATION: Friends who won't give, relatives who won't lend you a hand, avoid them like the plague.

96. Christmas Eve Dinner Starts at Noon

Christmas Eve dinner is a sacred event in any Guido home. Sure, dinner may start at noon, but your Nonnie and Mamma have been cooking for the past week. You get up early for a prosecco and orange juice cocktail and a slice of cold pizza. Dean Martin is singing all of the Christmas classics on the radio. The family (all forty of them) start to arrive at ten in the morning. The kids sing "Dominic the Donkey" while the adults break out the antipasto—cured olives, ham, peppers, snail salad, balls of mozzarella, sun-dried tomatoes, and bruschetta. Then comes the baccala (salted cod), along with the other traditional seven fishes. The truth is, you're glad this makes a once-a-year appearance. It's not your favorite Guido meal. In fact, most of the children (and adults really) push them under the bread and only pretend to eat them. With the baccala comes the fried calamari and shrimp. Then you get the pasta. Manicotti, ravioli, lasagna, baked ziti—stuffed pasta is the way to go! This grand feast goes on for hours. By this time Uncle Anthony has taken off his pants (never mind undoing one button, the amount of food in his stomach is serious). Your Pop is walking around the neighborhood smoking a cigar and trying to make room for the ricotta pie. You have time to stuff a piece of panetone in your face with a quick shot of espresso before you head out to midnight Mass. By the time your head hits the pillow, you don't know if you will ever eat again and you've been absolved of all of your sins. Not bad. Now get to sleep; Christmas day dinner is twice as long.

97. You Refer to Robert De Niro Only as "Bobby"

Robert De Niro—to you he's a god among men. He's not Robert to you
. . . he's Bobby. You feel like he's a close friend. He's the best damn
actor ever to grace the silver screen. If you saw him on the street,
you would cry and try to hold back from running into his arms. In *The
Godfather: Part II*, you marveled at his performance as a young Don
Corleone. You gained even more respect for him when seeing *Taxi
Driver* for the first time. As Jimmy Conway in *Goodfellas* he was more
than just a gangster, he was a legend. You even found him charming
in his more comedic roles in *Analyze This* and *Meet the Parents*. An
actor that can portray both violent, serious characters and older, wise-
cracking characters means a lot to you. On August 17 you buy a cake
and a few candles to wish Bobby a buon compleanno. When you found
out that he was battling prostate cancer, you held a candlelight vigil in
your backyard and prayed to the Virgin Mary to see him through it. If
you had one wish, it would be to have lunch with Bobby and talk about
every role he's ever played. Keep dreaming—you just might run into
him one day. But when you do, stick with Mr. De Niro.

GUESS THAT GANGSTER #15

This crime boss lived lavishly but was generally regarded as a cheapskate. He compelled members of his family to pay $25 a month in what were essentially union dues. He was also a devout Catholic who sought salvation through generous gifts to the church. The church accepted with a blind eye what was essentially blood money, as tainted as the thirty pieces of silver paid to Judas Iscariot. He was a rarity as far as dons go—he died of natural causes (cancer) while still head of his crime family. (See back of the book for the answer.)

YOU THINK YOU KNOW *GOODFELLAS*?

You claim you know every line from *Goodfellas*, that De Niro is your favorite actor, and that Scorsese is your hero. Think you know all there is to know about this classic? Take the quiz and find out.

1. Henry got pinched as a kid and learned a valuable lesson: "Never rat on your friends and keep your mouth shut." What did he get pinched for?

A. Selling cigarettes from a stolen truck

B. Stealing money from his neighbor

C. Stealing a car

D. Blowing up a building

2. On the day Henry gets arrested, he is running around town trying to fit everything in before sending Lois on a plane. What task does he have his brother do for the entire day?

A. Mow the lawn

B. Do the laundry

C. Stir the gravy

D. Paint the house

3. Tommy is upset that his girlfriend is prejudiced against Italians, especially because of her nationality. What nationality is she?

A. Lebanese

B. Iranian

C. African American

D. Jewish

4. During the scene where the bodies of all of the gangsters are being revealed, which Eric Clapton song is playing?

A. "Knockin' on Heaven's Door"

B. "Layla"

C. "Sunshine of Your Love"

D. "Cocaine"

5. After the major heist, Jimmy asks all involved not to buy anything extravagant for a while so they don't draw attention to themselves. Everyone does the exact opposite, and they spend their money wildly. What does Carbone buy for his wife?

A. A fur coat

B. A Cadillac

C. A diamond ring

D. A puppy

6. When Paulie and Henry have to go to jail, they are incarcerated in the same prison area. They still get to cook large dinners, so jail wasn't that much of a punishment. Paulie is in charge of the garlic. What does he use to cut the garlic?

A. A piece of glass

B. A shank

C. A sharpened toothbrush

D. A razor blade

7. Which club does Henry bring Karen to really impress her?

A. The Bamboo Club

B. The Crazy Horse

C. The Copacabana

D. The White Russian

8. After the big heist, where is Henry when he hears the news that it was successfully pulled off, making him one rich man?

A. In jail

B. In the shower

C. In bed with his mistress

D. At the grocery store

9. What is the name of the book that the movie is based on?
A. Wiseguy

B. Goodguys

C. Badguys

D. Funnyguys

10. How does Henry meet his wife Karen?
A. A blind double date

B. At the country club

C. In a restaurant

D. At the bakery

11. Karen throws a fit when she sees the name of Henry's girlfriend on the sign-in sheet when she visits him in prison. What is her name?
A. Maryann Grosso

B. Adriana La Cerva

C. Meredith Fanucci

D. Janice Rossi

12. Henry sets up connections for his side drug business in what city?
A. Miami

B. Pittsburgh

C. San Diego

D. Trenton

13. What is Jimmy Conway's favorite crime to commit?
A. Robbing banks

B. Murder

C. Hijacking trucks

D. Illegal gambling

14. Tommy gets heated when an old friend disrespects him at the bar in front of his girlfriend. He comes back later to kill him. What is that friend's name?

A. Jimmy Smits

B. Tommy Tutone

C. Billy Batts

D. Walt Johnson

15. What is the name of the big heist?

A. Lufthansa

B. Ludwig

C. Louis

D. Loneville

16. Tommy thinks he's about to get made when he's really going to get whacked. What did Tommy do to get killed?

A. He slept with the boss's wife.

B. He killed a made guy.

C. He burned down a made guy's house.

D. He stole from a made guy.

17. After he beats Karen's neighbor with a gun, what does Henry do with the weapon?

A. Hides it in his car

B. Leaves it with the neighbor

C. Gives it Karen to hide

D. Throws it in a drain

18. A lot of people get killed in *Goodfellas.* Which one of these characters doesn't get knocked off?

A. Jimmy

B. Tommy

C. Carbone

D. Morrie

19. At Henry and Karen's wedding, Karen notices that almost all of the guests have the same name. Which are the three names?

A. Louie, Lonnie, Marie

B. Timmy, Tommy, Angie

C. Paul, Tony, Jeannette

D. Peter, Paul, Marie

20. When Henry meets Karen's parents for the first time, she makes him do something before introducing him. What does she make him do?

A. Tuck in his shirt

B. Cover his cross

C. Take off his shoes

D. Put on a belt

21. When Henry is a kid his father gives him a beating for:

A. Disrespecting his mother

B. Hitting his younger sister

C. Missing so much school

D. Running with the wrong crowd

QUIZ ANSWERS

Answers: 1. A; **2.** C; **3.** D; **4.** B; **5.** A; **6.** D; **7.** C; **8.** B; **9.** A; **10.** A; **11.** D; **12.** B; **13.** C; **14.** C; **15.** A; **16.** B; **17.** C; **18.** A; **19.** D; **20.** B; **21.** C

GUESS THAT GANGSTER #16

He was a colorful gangster with leading-man looks and a way with the ladies. He was also aptly nicknamed. His nickname referred not only to the animated "screwy rabbit" but to his unbalanced mental state. Best buddies with Myer Lansky since childhood, the two little rascals formed an assassination bureau that preceded Murder Incorporated. Their friendship was tested when he went to Las Vegas and had a vision to turn the desert town into a gambling mecca. He went about making the dream a reality with messianic zeal. Unfortunately, his volatile temper and titanic ego got the better of him. His inflated budget and inability to take orders led to his murder, probably on the orders of his boyhood chum Lansky. He was a good-looking guy who had dreams of being a movie star, and he even had a movie star pal George Raft arrange a screen test. He never got his wish, but another movie star, Warren Beatty, played him in a 1991 film. (See back of the book for the answer.)

98. You Were the Only Kid in the Cafeteria to Have a Mortadella Sandwich for Lunch

Peanut butter and jelly, ham and cheese, tuna salad—any one of these sandwiches would have made you popular at the lunch table during your school years. However, being from a proud Italian family, you were left with the most questionable lunchmeat available—mortadella. If you glance quickly it just looks like a normal bologna and cheese sandwich. Look more closely and you see what makes it distinct—large white gobs of fat studded throughout. It can look a little scary to a seven-year-old. If you were really worried about getting ragged on, you just picked out the pieces of fat and told them it was Swiss bologna. Just wait until you have stuffed peppers or an eggplant grinder. They'll make you sit in the hall with that shit. Luckily for you, as a kid, mortadella was one of your favorite foods, so screw everyone else. They don't know what they're missing. Whip out the cannoli or pizzelle cookies your Ma packed for you and you'll have more friends than you can count—if you share.

99. You Danced with Your Father to "The Godfather Theme" at Your Wedding

You've dreamt about your wedding day since you were a little girl—daddy's little girl. When you saw *The Godfather* for the first time, you got choked up when Vito and Connie danced the traditional father-daughter dance among the five hundred friends and relatives in their backyard. When Connie throws her arms around her father's neck and waltzes slowly around the room, you knew that memory had to be replicated at your own wedding. You hired a special string quartet to play the theme to *The Godfather* while you and daddy danced. He cried more than you did during those four minutes of bliss. If you could only have gone back in time and hired Johnny Fontane to croon at the reception, everything would have been perfect.

100. You Mother Stayed Home from Work the Day Frank Sinatra Died

May 14, 1998, was a sad day in your house. Your mother didn't get out of her robe and slippers and laid on the couch crying and clutching her vinyl copy of Ol' Blue Eyes' greatest hits. She lit candles for him every Sunday at Mass while he was ill, and she went every hour on the hour on the day of his death. She gripped her rosary in a fierce attempt to pray for his immortal soul. Dinner wasn't on the table when Pop came home from work, and you had to order a pizza because Ma was just too distraught. She played "I've Got You Under My Skin" twenty times in a row while silently weeping. She even put in a tape of *Guys and Dolls*. It's been more than a decade, and even now when "Fly Me to the Moon" comes on the radio Ma has to leave the room. Sure, Frank was a great guy, but you'll never know what he meant to your Ma.

> **PAISANO Says**
>
> **Tony Soprano:** I can't watch this again.
> **Silvio Dante:** This is a DVD. It's the advanced bootleg.
> **Paulie Walnuts:** These are the alternative takes, Ton'.
> **Tony Soprano:** What, you gonna call Coppola and give ideas how to fix it?

101. You Don't Get Offended When Someone Calls You a Guido

In your world, being called a Guido isn't an insult. It's a compliment! There aren't many Italians who think like you. You are a rare breed. Many Italians find the word "guido" offensive. Italian organizations were quick to lash out against *The Sopranos* and *Jersey Shore* claiming they perpetuate a negative stereotype. You don't see what all the fuss is about. You're proud to call yourself a Guido and love everything that means. You're so proud, in fact, that you will scream "I'm a Guido!" down the street if the mood strikes you. You've turned a racial slur into a way of life and even made up the word "Guidette" so the ladies don't feel left out. Don't listen to the haters. You're not a disgratziat like some people say. Just don't call yourself a Guido in front of your grandmother or you'll get a smack in the head.

JERSEY SHORE SOUNDBITE

I was born and raised a Guido. It's just a lifestyle, it's being Italian, it's representing, family, friends, tanning, gel, everything.
—PAULY D

APPENDIX A:

TEN GUIDO RECIPES THAT WOULD MAKE YOUR NONNIE SAY "MANGIA, MANGIA!"

Escarole and Beans

INGREDIENTS
3 heads escarole
2 (16-ounce) cans cannellini beans
½ can water
Pepper, oregano, and garlic powder to taste
2 tablespoons olive oil
½–1 can chicken broth

INSTRUCTIONS

Cut the stems off the escarole and wash the pieces. Put the wet pieces into a pot, cover it, and put it on the stove on low to medium heat for about 15 minutes or until it becomes limp. Stir the leaves periodically. Once cooked, reduce heat to low.

In a separate pot, add the two cans of beans (do not rinse) and the water, using an empty can from the cannellini beans to measure. Add pepper, oregano, and garlic powder, along with 2 tablespoons olive oil. Cook on stove until it boils.

Drain excess water from escarole and add the beans with the chicken broth and let simmer for ten to fifteen minutes.

Let sit overnight for thickness, or add pasta if you would like.

Vodka Sauce

INGREDIENTS

½ stick butter

¼ cup vodka

¼ teaspoon Worcestershire sauce

1 cup marinara sauce

1 cup half-and-half

INSTRUCTIONS

Melt butter in a small saucepan. Add vodka and Worcestershire sauce and heat until it bubbles. Slowly add the marinara sauce and half-and-half and cook until creamy.

Meatballs

INGREDIENTS
1 pound ground beef
1 egg
¼ cup breadcrumbs
2 slices bread, made mushy with water
¼ cup water
Pinch salt, pepper, and garlic powder

INSTRUCTIONS
Mix all ingredients together and separate into 1- to 2-inch balls. Place on pan and bake for 5 minutes under the broiler.

Baked Ziti

INGREDIENTS
1 pound ziti
1 quart Bolognese sauce (see recipe)
1 small mozzarella ball, chopped into cubes
1 small container ricotta cheese
1 cup Pecorino Romano cheese, grated

INSTRUCTIONS

Boil the ziti until cooked al dente, then drain. Add ½ quart Bolognese sauce, followed by the mozzarella and half the ricotta. Add ¼ of the Romano cheese. Place in a 9" x 13" Pyrex dish. Add the remaining sauce and cheese on the top. Bake at 350°F for 25–30 minutes.

Bolognese Sauce

INGREDIENTS
1 small onion
3 cloves garlic
1–2 tablespoons extra-virgin olive oil
1 pound chopped ground beef
2 35-ounce cans peeled, whole plum tomatoes with basil
2 8-ounce cans tomato sauce
Salt and pepper to taste
1 teaspoon sugar
Splash red wine

INSTRUCTIONS

Chop the onion and 3 cloves garlic; sauté in 3-quart saucepan over medium heat with 1–2 tablespoons olive oil until golden brown. Do not burn. Add 1 pound ground beef and sauté over medium heat until brown. Drain the fat.

Put the peeled, whole plum tomatoes with basil in a blender and crush. Pour into meat mixture. Add the 2 cans tomato sauce. Add salt, pepper, sugar, and a splash of red wine to taste. Cook over medium-low heat for about 1 hour.

Pasta Fagioli

INGREDIENTS

1 small onion, sliced

4 cloves garlic, sliced

2 tablespoons extra-virgin olive oil

1 8-ounce can tomato sauce

Salt and pepper to taste

1 19-ounce can cannellini beans

1 19-ounce can water (use the empty cannellini bean can)

Oregano, salt, and pepper to taste

½ pound small pasta of choice

INSTRUCTIONS

Heat sliced onion and garlic in olive oil in a small frying pan over medium heat. Brown the garlic, but do not let it burn; it should be a light brown color. Add tomato sauce into frying pan and heat for about 10 minutes. Add salt and pepper to taste. Remove the garlic slices.

In a separate 1-quart saucepan, add the cannellini beans. Fill the empty cannellini bean can with water and pour into saucepan. Cook on medium heat until the beans begin to boil for approximately 5–10 minutes. Add salt, pepper, and oregano to taste. Add the tomato sauce to the pot with the beans, et voilà! Hint: Reserve about ½ cup of the beans and purée them in a blender and then add that to the sauce to make it a little bit thicker.

In a separate pot, cook pasta al dente. Drain pasta and pour bean mixture into pasta. Stir it and serve.

Zucchini Pie

INGREDIENTS
3 cups chopped zucchini (3 zucchini)
1 small onion, chopped
4 large eggs
1 cup Bisquik
½ cup vegetable oil
½ cup grated cheese
1 cup shredded Jarlsberg cheese
1 teaspoon parsley
½ teaspoon marjoram
½ teaspoon salt and pepper

INSTRUCTIONS

Mix all ingredients well. Pour into buttered rectangular pan. Bake at 350°F for 40–45 minutes until golden.

Chicken Parmigiana

INGREDIENTS
1 pound chicken cutlets
2–3 eggs
Splash milk
1 cup flavored breadcrumbs
1 pint marinara sauce (see recipe)
4 ounces mozzarella cheese

INSTRUCTIONS

Clean the chicken cutlets. Break eggs and mix in a bowl with a splash of milk. In a separate bowl, put in flavored breadcrumbs. Soak cutlets in eggs, and then dip each cutlet in breadcrumbs. Fry on both sides in a large frying pan until golden brown. Cover the bottom of a 13" x 16" baking dish with marinara sauce. Place cutlets in baking dish. Slice mozzarella cheese and place on top of each cutlet. Cover cutlets with remaining marinara sauce. Bake until cheese is melted, 15–20 minutes at about 375°F.

Marinara Sauce

INGREDIENTS

1 small onion

2–3 cloves garlic

1–2 tablespoons extra-virgin olive oil

2 35-ounce cans peeled plum-shaped tomatoes with basil

1 8-ounce can tomato sauce

Salt and pepper to taste

1 teaspoon sugar

Splash red wine

2 basil leaves (optional)

INSTRUCTIONS

Sauté onion and garlic in oil in a large frying pan until lightly brown. Blend the plum tomatoes in a blender to crush. Add the blended tomatoes and the tomato sauce to the onions, garlic, and oil. Sauté and add salt, pepper, sugar, and red wine. Crush another clove of garlic in the bubbling sauce and cook for 30–45 minutes until thick. Add two basil leaves when cooking.

Sausage and Peppers

INGREDIENTS
4 large red, green, or mixed peppers, sliced
1 large onion, sliced
2 tablespoons plus 1 teaspoon olive oil
Pinch salt and pepper
8 sausage links

INSTRUCTIONS
Slice peppers and onions. Sauté in 2 tablespoons oil in a medium frying pan on a low to medium heat until tender. Add a pinch of salt and pepper. Cook sausage in a separate pan with a teaspoon of oil on a low flame until cooked through. Combine sausage with peppers and onions into one pan and serve.

ANSWERS TO GUESS
THAT GANGSTER

1. Joseph Bonanno

2. Salvatore "Bill" Bonanno

3. Alphonse "Scarface" Capone

4. Paul Castellano

5. Joseph Columbo Sr.

6. Frank Costello

7. Carmine Galante

8. Carlo Gambino

9. Vito Genovese

10. Sam "Momo" Giancana

11. Vincent "The Chin" Gigante

12. John Gotti

13. Sammy "The Bull" Gravano

14. Charles "Lucky" Luciano

15. Joseph Profaci

16. Benjamin "Bugsy" Siegel

ABOUT THE AUTHORS

Andrea Renzoni is a book publishing professional, author, and lover of all things Italian. Her favorite movie is *The Godfather*. Her favorite food is eggplant Parmesan. She lives with her fiancé and two cats in a neighborhood in Rhode Island that smells of garlic every Sunday.

Eric Renzoni graduated from Bridgewater State College with a bachelor's degree in criminal justice. He hopes to one day be a police officer, but at the moment he lives with his cat in a one-bedroom apartment, bartending and doing odd jobs (such as writing books about Guidos) to make ends meet. This is the first book he has written, but he hopes that more offers come his way for other projects in the future.

ART CREDITS

Printed in the United States
By Bookmasters